REINHOLD PLASTICS
APPLICATIONS SERIES

ACRYLIC RESINS

by

MILTON B. HORN
Catalin Corporation of America

REINHOLD PUBLISHING CORPORATION

NEW YORK

CHAPMAN & HALL, LTD., LONDON

Copyright © 1960 by
REINHOLD PUBLISHING CORPORATION

———————

Library of Congress Catalog Card Number: 60-8707

Printed in the United States of America

Reinhold Plastics
Applications Series

This series was started in 1957 with sixteen titles in prospect. The present volume on Acrylic Resins is the fourteenth of the series. However, the series has been lengthened as new plastics materials have appeared on the scene, and seven more books are now in preparation. These include volumes on polyesters, polystyrene, polycarbonates and polypropylene.

The theme of the series is guidance in application. The optimum application of a plastic in a very real sense determines its true worth. Most of the books in the series describe the properties, the chemistry and the application of a single plastic or of a single family of plastics. A few describe fabrications of plastics.

The books are semi-technical—that is, one does not need to be a research chemist to understand the various volumes. The authors have kept in mind as probable readers such industrial men and women as design engineers, equipment manufacturers, producers of packages, manufacturers of packaging machinery, students at technical schools and, of course, all people in the plastics industry—material manufacturers, molders, extruders, fabricators.

In addition to the above, it is hoped that each title will appeal to readers in specialized categories. Plastics from which fibers are made may be of interest to tire and fabric manufacturers. One book, for instance, may describe materials favorable for production of sheets used for handbags and luggage. Similarly, other titles may appeal to manufacturers of paints, magnetic tapes, upholstery, plywood and furniture.

With the series now about two-thirds complete, and with encouragement from its wide acceptance in industry, it is with enthusiasm that this fourteenth book is presented.

HERBERT R. SIMONDS, *Editor*

PREFACE

Acrylic resins, in one or another form, have found their way into most of our homes, factories, commercial buildings and vehicles. The purpose of this book is to classify these resins as to basic types and then to give full application information. Data are included on the raw materials and manufacturing processes used in making the resins, to provide the user with a better understanding of the product with which he is concerned.

The rate of growth of the plastics industry over the past twenty-five years has precluded the possibility of any one person having a comprehensive knowledge of more than a very few facets of the industry. A person will usually concentrate on one phase. He may be an emulsion chemist, a textile applications man or a sales engineer. The businessman and the technical man will find this book of value as it gives a bird's-eye view of the industry.

The book is, of necessity, general in nature. However, a little generalization in this age of specialization may help to broaden our horizons.

The author wishes to acknowledge the many industrial organizations that patiently answered his many queries and permitted the use of their charts, tables and illustrations. Thanks are due to Mr. Joseph B. Hyman and Mr. Stanley Kordzinski for their assistance, and to Mr. Robert Raetz for his help in gathering information on suspension polymerization.

MILTON B. HORN

Warren Township, New Jersey
January, 1960

TITLES PUBLISHED

Amino Resins, *John F. Blais*

Cellulosics, *Walter Paist*

Epoxy Resins, *Irving Skeist*

Fluorocarbons, *Merritt A. Rudner*

Gum Plastics, *M. Stafford Thompson*

Laminated Plastics, *D. J. Duffin*

Phenolics, *David F. Gould*

Plastic Sheet Forming, *Robert L. Butzko*

Polyamide Resins, *Don E. Floyd*

Polyethylene, *Theodore O. J. Kresser*

Polyurethanes, *Bernard A. Dombrow*

Silicones, *Robert N. Meals and Frederick M. Lewis*

Vinyl Resins, *W. Mayo Smith*

CONTENTS

Page

INTRODUCTION iii

PREFACE v

Chapter

1. INTRODUCTION 1

2. CHEMISTRY OF ACRYLIC MONOMERS AND
   POLYMERS 14

3. CAST ACRYLICS: MANUFACTURE AND PROPERTIES 33

4. FABRICATION AND APPLICATION OF CAST
   ACRYLICS 51

5. MOLDING POWDERS: THEIR MANUFACTURE
   AND USE 84

6. ACRYLIC EMULSIONS: MANUFACTURE . . . 101

7. MANUFACTURE OF SOLUTION POLYMERS . . 114

8. APPLICATIONS OF EMULSIONS AND SOLUTIONS . 123

9. MISCELLANEOUS ACRYLIC MONOMERS AND
   APPLICATIONS 149

10. FUTURE TRENDS 163

    APPENDIX: SELECTED READING MATERIAL . . 176

    INDEX 180

1. INTRODUCTION

The acrylic monomers are a group of synthetic chemicals that form a sub-order of the parent group of vinyl-type monomers. When these vinyl-type monomers are polymerized, they yield a large and varied group of thermoplastic materials that have found widespread use. Recent estimates show that 60 per cent of all synthetic resin and plastic production in the United States is based on these vinyl-type polymers.

THE VINYL FAMILY

The vinyl grouping that is common to all these monomers is $CH_2=C\big\langle$. This group combines with other radicals in various ways to yield some of our most common plastics.

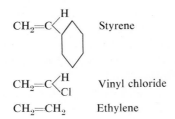

$$CH_2=C\big\langle \begin{array}{c} H \\ \end{array} \quad \text{Styrene}$$

$$CH_2=C\big\langle \begin{array}{c} H \\ Cl \end{array} \quad \text{Vinyl chloride}$$

$$CH_2=CH_2 \quad \text{Ethylene}$$

Other members of the group are vinylidene compounds, isobutylene, chloroprene and many others.

When an acid or carboxyl group is joined to the vinyl radical together with an H or CH_3 the products are acrylic and methacrylic acids. These are the chemical starting points for all acrylic plastics.

$$CH_2=C\begin{array}{c}H\\COOH\end{array}\quad \text{Acrylic acid}$$

$$CH_2=C\begin{array}{c}CH_3\\COOH\end{array}\quad \text{Methacrylic acid}$$

It should be noted that, except for ethylene, the other monomers listed are structurally unsymmetrical. The vinyl polymers have an amorphous rather than crystalline structure and they are quite easily formed at elevated temperatures.

Esterification of the acrylic acids with various alcohol substituents gives the large group of acrylic esters with a wide range of properties dependent upon the chain length of the alcohol used. Halogen substitution yields another large group of useful acrylates of which the chloroacrylates are best known. The nitrogen-containing acrylics have also had widespread use. Best known of these is acrylonitrile. Acrylamide and acrylaldehyde (acrolein) and many derivatives are also available commercially.

The acrylic monomers are used as intermediates in the synthesis of many organic compounds. In the preparation of plastics, our interest is in their ability to polymerize through the double carbon-to-carbon bond. This polymerization is generally peroxide-catalyzed. Heat and light alone will polymerize acrylics, but this is rarely done on a commercial scale. Anionic catalysts will also produce polymers, but this reaction too is not used commercially.

Depending on the purpose to which the product is to be put, a number of different types of polymerization are used. Bulk polymerization is used for cast sheet, rods and tubes. Suspension polymerization is the usual method for the production of molding powders, and the emulsion and solution techniques are used to yield polymers in forms convenient for coating and impregnation.

GENERAL PROPERTIES AND PRODUCTS

Acrylic polymers cover a wide range of physical properties. Depending on the monomers selected and the method of polymerization, the product can be anything from a viscous, oily material to a tough and rigid sheet. Because of this range, acrylics are adapted to almost every application where plastics are used. All the acrylics have an unusual degree of resistance to the effects of long exposure to sunlight, heat and weathering. In this respect they are much superior to such related materials as styrene, vinyl chloride, vinyl acetate, and also to cellulose acetate. For this reason, acrylics are generally chosen for outdoor purposes.

Another interesting property of acrylics is the clarity of films and sheets produced from methyl methacrylate. Cast sheet produced by bulk polymerization in cells makes the best of synthetic glass-like plastics. It is rigid, tough, can easily be formed by the fabricator and has fairly high impact strength. It displays excellent weatherability and easily accepts dyes and pigments. It is produced in transparent form, both clear and colored, and either translucent or opaque. The major fault with cast acrylic sheet is its low resistance to surface scratching. It also shows a tendency to craze under stress and is affected by organic solvents. Much work has been done to improve the properties of cast sheet, and the recent innovation of biaxial stretching has improved resistance to both crazing and shattering. Cast sheet, rod, and tube are major materials for outdoor signs and displays. Acrylic sheet is used in the aircraft field for windshields, canopies and instrument covers. Use is growing in the architectural field for decorative panels, skylights and glazing.

The same qualities inherent in cast methyl methacrylate sheet also hold true for products made by injection molding with acrylic molding powder. A number of different grades of injection-molding powders are available, differing mainly in their heat resistance. These molding powders are manufactured by suspension polymerization followed by extrusion into rods. The rods are then chopped into pellets of convenient

The outdoor testing of cast sheet is done continuously to assure that the colors used will stand up as well as the sheet itself. (*Courtesy of The Rohm & Haas Reporter, August 1959.*)

size. Under controlled conditions the product is of high molecular weight within a narrow range. Some of the many products made by injection molding of acrylics are automotive stop light covers, knobs, dials, instrument panels, TV masks and shields, and brush handles.

Extruded products are also made from molding powder. Thin acrylic sheet can be extruded but it does not have as good properties as cast sheet. Rods, tubes and decorative items for display work are made by extrusion. High-impact molding powder has recently been introduced for the shoe-heel industry. The heels can be nailed without splitting.

Many of the newer synthetic fibers are based on the nitrogen-substituted acrylic, acrylonitrile. These fibers, when made into garments and fabrics, exhibit resistance to aging, moisture and sunlight. Because of their moisture resistance and high wet strength they can be easily washed. Acrylonitrile is also used as a modifier of cotton to give it improved properties. Blends of polyacrylonitrile with acetate and rayon produce fabrics with good dyeing properties and interesting textures.

Acrylonitrile has been used for making elastomeric materials with improved properties. It is highly superior to the standard GR-S rubber with respect to flex-life and in its resistance to oxidation and sunlight. It is, however, inferior to GR-S in tensile strength. Acrylonitrile-butadiene rubbers enjoy wide usage where heat and oil resistance are critical. An example of this application is for the gaskets in automatic transmissions for automobiles. Acrylonitrile is also used to replace part of the styrene in GR-S rubber-making, a widely used tripolymer product known as ABS. These various rubbers are manufactured by emulsion polymerization, followed by precipitation of the latex.

Emulsion polymerization has also been used to create an extensive series of acrylic polymers and copolymers used in the treatment of textiles. Permanent stiffeners of acrylic emulsions are used to replace starching. Other emulsions forming soft films have been used to "body" fabrics and give them a soft, full hand. Emulsions have been useful in the binding of non-woven fabrics and for the backing of upholstery, rugs and pile fabrics.

Water-soluble polymers have been used for thickeners and sizings. These include polyacrylic acid and its salts and poly-acrylamide. Nylon is usually sized with water-soluble acrylic polymers before weaving for ease in handling and prevention of snagging. The size is later removed from the finished article by scouring.

The coating of paper is another field where acrylic emulsions have proved their value. The emulsion is compounded with clay and pigment, which is roll- or knife-coated onto the paper. The paper is dried and then calendered. The resulting finish is grease-resistant and has excellent gloss. If the compounding is done with sufficient acrylic binder the printing quality is excellent.

Although a comparative newcomer in the field, acrylics have been making great strides in the field of emulsion-based paints. Although the volume has not been as large as the vinyls because of the price factor, the acrylics are superior for the purpose. They are easy to apply, dry rapidly and are free from odor. They have also been recommended for exterior as well as interior use and can be applied over such difficult-to-paint surfaces as concrete and cinder block, even when damp.

Products made by polymerization in organic solvents, known as solution polymers, find many specialty uses in the lacquer and coatings field, and as pressure-sensitive and heat-sealing adhesives. The water-white lacquers are usually acrylic solution polymers. Their outstanding clarity and resistance to aging is demonstrated by the fact that they are used in the renovation and protection of art treasures. Depending on the monomers used in the polymer, the films can range from soft and tacky to hard and brittle.

One of the important features that makes acrylic polymers

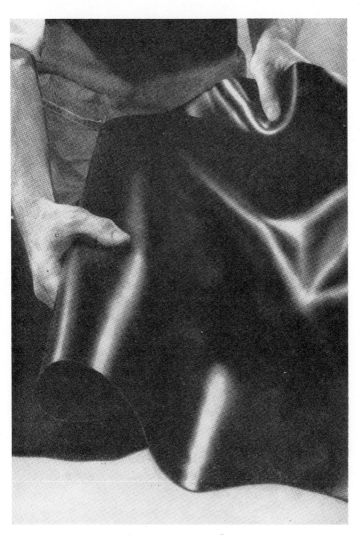

The acrylic emulsion base coat adds to the "hand" and "roundness" of an upholstery leather. It must also be tested for adhesion to the leather and crack resistance in cold weather. (*Courtesy of The Rohm & Haas Reporter, August 1959.*)

desirable as coating is that no plasticizer is needed to produce
a soft film. Acrylics are spoken of as being internally plasticized by use, in desired proportion, of the normally soft
monomers in their preparation. Plasticizer is efficient as a
softening agent, but tends to migrate to the surface, giving
the plastic a greasy feel, and eventually loss of plasticizer in
coatings causes embrittlement that leads to failure. Internally
plasticized acrylics will retain their softness indefinitely. The
use of solution polymers of acrylics as a coating material for
raincoats points up this property.

The field of leather finishing uses acrylics in both emulsion
and solution form. Pigmented and compounded emulsions
are used extensively as base coats that anchor to the leather.
Acrylic lacquers are frequently used as top coatings for
leather.

Emulsions and solutions are used widely in the specialty
adhesive field. They may be formulated for pressure-sensitive,
laminating and heat-sealing adhesives and are used in cases
where clarity is desirable and where failure due to aging is
to be avoided.

Other interesting uses for acrylics cover such miscellaneous
items as resins for soil stabilization, dental restorations, embedment of specimens for permanent microscope slides and
demonstrations.

Evaluation of acrylics for other uses is in process of
development. Recent work has been done in their use as soil
stabilizers, and as a molding material for reinforced plastics
of the fiber-glass-polyester type.

COST CONSIDERATIONS

This introduction to the forms in which acrylic polymers
are available and comment on some of their more common
applications gives an understanding of the versatility of the

plastic and its excellent properties. However, it leaves un-answered the question of why total sales of acrylics in all forms is but a small portion of total plastics sales. In 1957 sales of acrylics totaled about 100,000,000 pounds—less than 2 per cent of total sales of synthetic resins and plastics.

The answer lies within the price structure in the plastics industry. The deterrent that has limited a wider use of acrylic lies in the price of the monomers. The least expensive, acrylo-nitrile, is presently priced at 19¢ a pound. The least expensive of the acrylic esters is methyl methacrylate, at 29¢ a pound. Ethyl acrylate is 34¢ a pound, and the prices range upward for the more common esters to 55¢ a pound. This is in sharp contrast to styrene at about 12¢ and vinyl chloride at 12½¢ a pound.

In spite of this price difference, the sale of acrylics has been enjoying a steady rise from year to year, and recently a number of new monomer plants have been built by estab-lished companies that have entered the field. These new plants and the competitive situation in monomers have resulted in recent price drops in monomer butyl acrylate and ethyl-hexyl acrylate (soft and tacky polymers), dropping from 55¢ to 40¢ a pound and acrylic acid, dropping in one jump from $1.14 to 64¢.

COPOLYMERS

Although homopolymers are used in some cases, most acrylics are copolymers of 2, 3, or 4 monomers. Even cast sheet, while essentially made of methyl methacrylate, usually has a small portion of methacrylic acid or perhaps some cross-linking agent. Resins for paper coating, emulsion paints and textile treating are usually a combination of varying pro-portions of ethyl acrylate and methyl methacrylate, these being the least expensive of the acrylic esters.

Many resins listed as acrylic copolymers may have some

minor proportion of vinyl acetate or styrene in their composition. This may be done to lower the cost or perhaps to improve the properties of a resin for a specific end use. Acrylics are also added in lesser quantities because of their ability to help other monomers to polymerize. In other cases many vinyl base resins contain some portion of an acrylic ester that serves to upgrade the product. Many vinyl co-polymers fall into this group.

The vinyls and their sub-order, acrylics, are all classified as thermoplastic materials that can be repeatedly softened by heating. This is ideal for the fabricator who can heat and form products that will retain this form when they have been cooled. However, this heat softening is too often a feature that is not desirable in the finished product. For this reason much work has been done to add a degree of thermosetting property to acrylics. Some moldability is lost in the process, but the improvement in heat resistance offsets this. Emulsions often use a proportion of a cross-linking agent to increase the heat and solvent resistance of the resin.

MONOMER AND POLYMER SOURCES

Acrylics are not in any sense a new plastic. Their industrial history dates back to 1927 when the German firm of Rohm & Haas first produced polymethyl acrylate under the name "Acryloid." This was a solution polymer in an organic solvent and it was suggested for use in lacquers and surface coatings. The laboratory history of acrylics dates back to 1843 when acrylic acid was first synthesized. By 1900, most of the common acrylates were known in the laboratory and many of the basic factors involved in polymerization were understood. Consistent work on the part of Dr. Otto Rohm, starting in 1901, led to the formation of the firm of Rohm & Haas and the commercial exploitation of the acrylates.

Starting at a later date, Rowland Hill, of the British firm, Imperial Chemical Industries, worked with the methacrylic esters and evolved the commercial process for the manufacture of cast sheet.

Until recently, the manufacture of acrylic ester monomers was done only by Rohm & Haas. Increased demand and new basic processes for manufacture brought others into the field. Now acrylic esters are available from Union Carbide as well as from Celanese. Acrylic acid is available from these companies and also Goodrich Chemical Co. Methacrylic acid and esters are sold by both Rohm & Haas and DuPont.

The major sources for acrylonitrile are American Cyanamid and Union Carbide; acrylamide is produced by American Cyanamid; acrolein is available from both Union Carbide and Shell Chemical. Many of the substituted acrylics are produced in industrial quantities and are available from a number of sources among which are Union Carbide, Rohm & Haas, Borden, etc. European producers of monomers are Imperial Chemical of England and Rohm & Haas of Germany. These two companies supply the European market and export a part of their production to many parts of the world. ICI is supplying Canadian needs through their representative, Canadian Industries, Ltd. United States producers export to some extent and importation to this country is a bare minimum.

While acrylic monomers are available from only a limited number of sources, the list of producers of polymers is quite extensive. It ranges from our largest producers of chemicals to small enterprises producing specialty items. Cast methacrylate sheet is made by Rohm & Haas under the trade name "Plexiglas." Their production accounts for the largest part of the market. Four or five smaller producers account for the balance of the sheet produced and, in the main, their products are specialty and decorative sheet. Two of these producers use a goodly portion of their product for captive purposes.

Until a few years ago, DuPont also produced cast sheet, rods and tubes. Rod and tube production was continued by Cadillac Plastics, who also specialize in massive castings. Molding

This military aircraft will be assured of excellent weatherability by a sprayed finish of lacquer based on an acrylic solution polymer. (*Courtesy of The Rohm & Haas Reporter, August 1959.*)

powder in various grades is available from DuPont under the name of "Lucite" and from Rohm & Haas, as "Plexiglas."

Solution polymers are produced in quantity by Rohm & Haas under the name of "Acryloid." Many other companies produce acrylic solutions for specialty purposes ranging from adhesives to lacquers. There is a tendency for users of polymers to avoid the use of solutions because of their highly flammable nature due to the solvent and also the cost factor involved in loss of this solvent. Nevertheless, in many instances the solution polymer is best for the application. An example of this is where there is a need for the best possible water resistance.

Rohm & Haas' "Rhoplexes" are the leading group of products in the field of emulsion polymers. In the last few years, many other companies have entered the field. Among these are Borden, Polyvinyl Chemicals, Catalin, Reichhold, Staley, and others. In Europe, the Badische Anilin und Soda Fabrik have a long history of emulsion manufacture, as has ICI in England. In Belgium, the producer is the Union Chemique Belge. France and Italy also have their producers of acrylic emulsions.

All four major rubber producers in the United States also have a line of acrylic rubbers based on polymers of acrylonitrile-butadiene. Goodrich products are named "Hycar." Goodyear latices are called "Chemigum." The Naugatuck Division of the United States Rubber Co. makes "Kralastik" rubbers. Many of these products are tripolymers of acrylonitrile-styrene-butadiene.

The water-soluble acrylic polymers comprise another group that have numerous uses. These are the polymers of acrylic and methacrylic acid and their sodium and ammonium salts. The "Acrysols" of Rohm & Haas, polymethacrylic acid of DuPont, and the polyacrylamides of American Cyanamid are in this category. They are sold as rather viscous solutions or in easily soluble dry form.

2. CHEMISTRY OF ACRYLIC MONOMERS AND POLYMERS

The process through which we have come to understand the basic chemistry of acrylics has followed the classical pattern so characteristic of scientific growth and development. First there is the long period of gathering of unrelated facts in the laboratories. Then, through the efforts of an individual or a small group, these facts, now available in sizable number, are related to one another in a systematic fashion. This leads to the introduction of the first reliable theory. This, in turn, stimulates accelerated laboratory activity to fill in the gaps in the theory, and a solid body of knowledge begins to reach maturity.

At this point, commercial possibilities are investigated. If they are found and exploited by the development chemist and engineer, then what was a laboratory curiosity soon becomes a group of well known terms in the never-ending list of trade names.

HISTORICAL BACKGROUND

Over 100 years ago the preparation of acrylic acid was reported by the oxidation of acrolein (acrylic aldehyde). The acrolein was made by the dry distillation of glycerine. It was almost thirty years after this discovery before another observer noted the polymerization of the acid, but with little understanding of what had taken place. Before the turn of

14

the century, laboratory methods were devised for the preparation of many of the lower acrylates and methacrylates. Data on polymerization were becoming of sizable volume and included such detailed information as the inhibiting effect of oxygen. In 1901, Dr. Rohm in his doctoral dissertation, brought this information into a single document and laid the foundations for the theoretical understanding that led to further progress.

Rohm persisted in his work and in 1914 was issued a U.S. Patent for the production of acrylic esters from lactic acid. In 1927 the firm of Rohm & Haas A. G. started the production of polymethyl acrylate under the trade names of "Acryloid" and "Plexigum." At the same time Imperial Chemical Industries of England, under the leadership of Rowland Hill, solved the problems of production of methacrylic esters. This led to the first commercial bulk castings of methyl methacrylate, and the name "Perspex" came into being.

Throughout the years, many laboratory methods of synthesizing monomers have been suggested. The bulk of these methods, when put to the test of commercially feasible and economical production, were discarded. At the present time, the commercial production of the acrylics use such low cost materials as acetone, ethylene, ethylene oxide, cyanides, sulfuric acid, acetylene, methanol, ethanol, and other alcohols.

MONOMER CHEMISTRY

Acrylic chemistry starts with the basic acrylic formula:

$$CH_2 = C \begin{smallmatrix} R' \\ COO(R) \end{smallmatrix}$$

This formula characterizes the chemical as a vinyl type monomer capable of undergoing a number of molecular changes. The double bond between the first two carbons indicates that it will polymerize in chains to form thermoplastic resins. The R and R′ can be replaced by the aliphatic series CH_3, C_2H_5, etc. to yield a long series of materials with varying properties. If both R and R′ are hydrogens we have acrylic acid. If R′ is a CH_3 group we have methacrylic acid:

$$CH_2{=}CH{-}COOH$$
acrylic acid

$$CH_2{=}\overset{\overset{\textstyle CH_3}{\textstyle |}}{C}{-}COOH$$
methacrylic acid

Replacing R with CH_3 yields methyl acrylate or methyl methacrylate:

$$CH_2{=}CH{-}COO{-}CH_3$$
methyl acrylate

$$CH_2{=}\overset{\overset{\textstyle CH_3}{\textstyle |}}{C}{-}COO{-}CH_3$$
methyl methacrylate

When a CN or nitrile group replaces the carboxyl we get:

$$CH_2{=}CH{-}CN$$
acrylonitrile

The NH_2 or amide group gives acrylamide and replacement of the carboxyl with the aldehyde, CHO, group yields acrolein, or acrylaldehyde:

$$CH_2{=}CH{-}CO{-}NH_2$$
acrylamide

$$CH_2{=}CH{-}CHO$$
acrolein

Either the R or R′ or both may be replaced by a halide, an acid halide, or many other groups in various combinations, giving rise to a large class of compounds. Some of these are commercial and some are only laboratory products.

The Monomer-Polymer division of the Borden Co. lists 161 acrylic and methacrylic monomers in its catalog. The large majority of these compounds are offered for laboratory evaluations. These materials are manufactured in pilot plant quantities and are priced as high as $50.00 per pound in some cases. As new uses are found for these materials and they are produced in commercial quantity, their price will be lowered in proportion. These materials are mainly higher homologs of industrially available monomers and various substituted acrylics. The substituted compounds may be of the nitrogen, halogen, cyclic, aryl and alkyl-aryl types.

ACRYLIC ACID

$$CH_2{=}CHCOOH$$

	Physical Properties (Glacial Form)
Molecular weight	72.06
Specific gravity, 20/20°C	1.052
Boiling point °C, 760 mm Hg	140.9
Vapor pressure, mm Hg at 20°C	3.1
Freezing point, °C	12.1
Ionization constant, K, at 25°C	0.000055
Solubility in water, 20°C	Complete
of water in, 20°C	Complete
Weight per gallon, 20°C, lb	8.6

COMMERCIAL SYNTHESIS

A knowledge of the commercial methods for the production of the common monomers will lead to an understanding of how most of the acrylics can be synthesized.

Methyl methacrylate was first synthesized commercially by the acetone-cyanohydrin process. Acetone was reacted with hydrogen cyanide or sodium cyanide in the presence of potassium hydroxide to yield acetone-cyanohydrin. This was further reacted with sulfuric acid. With the aid of heat this produced crude methacrylamide sulfate. Reacting this with methanol and water yielded methyl methacrylate and ammonium bisulfate:

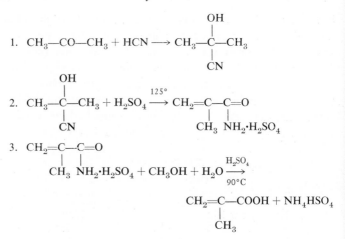

1. $CH_3—CO—CH_3 + HCN \longrightarrow CH_3—\overset{\overset{\displaystyle OH}{|}}{\underset{\underset{\displaystyle CN}{|}}{C}}—CH_3$

2. $CH_3—\overset{\overset{\displaystyle OH}{|}}{\underset{\underset{\displaystyle CN}{|}}{C}}—CH_3 + H_2SO_4 \overset{125°}{\longrightarrow} CH_2{=}\underset{\underset{\displaystyle CH_3}{|}}{C}—\underset{\underset{\displaystyle NH_2·H_2SO_4}{|}}{C}{=}O$

3. $CH_2{=}\underset{\underset{\displaystyle CH_3}{|}}{C}—\underset{\underset{\displaystyle NH_2·H_2SO_4}{|}}{C}{=}O + CH_3OH + H_2O \overset{H_2SO_4}{\underset{90°C}{\longrightarrow}}$

$$CH_2{=}\underset{\underset{\displaystyle CH_3}{|}}{C}—COOH + NH_4HSO_4$$

Distillation of the product at reduced pressure gave a very pure monomer. This is the method used now by all producers of methyl methacrylate.

Methyl acrylate can be synthesized commercially by reacting ethylene oxide with hydrogen cyanide to yield ethylene cyanohydrin. This is further reacted with methanol and sulfuric acid to yield methyl acrylate and ammonium bisulfate.

1. $CH_2\overset{\diagdown}{\underset{\diagup}{}}CH_2 + HCN \longrightarrow OH—CH_2{=}CH_2—CN$
O

2. $OH—CH_2—CH_2—CN + CH_3OH + H_2SO_4 \longrightarrow$

$$CH_2{=}CH—COOCH_3 + NH_4HSO_4$$

Esters of the higher alcohols can be produced by the above processes if the higher alcohol is substituted for the methanol. Higher acrylates can also be made by alcoholysis or transesterification in which the lower alkyl is substituted by a higher group. Good yields are obtained by this method using a catalyst such as toluene-sulfonic acid. Ethyl acrylate is preferred to the methyl in this process because of its higher

An acrylic monomer plant. Consistently high standards of product purity are essential to the manufacture of duplicable polymers. (*Courtesy of The Rohm & Haas Reporter, August 1959.*)

PHYSICAL CONSTANTS OF THE THREE MOST COMMONLY USED
ACRYLIC ESTER MONOMERS

Properties	Methyl Acrylate	Ethyl Acrylate	Methyl Methacrylate
Molecular weight	86	100	100
Boiling point, °C	79.6-80.3	99.3-99.7	100.6-101.1
Freezing point, °C	< -75	< -75	-48.2
Refractive index (N_d at 25°C)	1.401	1.404	1.412
Specific gravity, 25°/25°C	0.952	0.919	0.940
Flash point, °F			
Closed cup, Tagliabue	26.6	48.2	50.0
Open cup, Cleveland	60	85	85
Viscosity, cs at 25°C	0.503	0.596	0.569
Vapor pressure: mm Hg at			
2°C	. .	21	18
10	46	27	24
20	72	40	35
30	112	61	53
40	177	93	81
50	270	142	124
60	395	210	189
70	565	300	279
80	765	425	397
90	. .	582	547
95	. .	. .	. .
Solubility in water at 30°C, % by wt	5.2	1.82	1.50
Heat of polymerization, kcal/mole	19-20	. .	13
Density, lb/gal	7.95	7.65	7.8

boiling point. It is also necessary to add a polymerization inhibitor such as hydroquinone. Acrylonitrile is also a good starting material for the synthesis of the higher acrylic esters. In this case the acrylonitrile is hydrolyzed and reacted with the higher alcohol. The methods stated also hold true for the higher methacrylic esters, using as starting materials a lower methacrylic ester or methacrylonitrile.

PHYSICAL PROPERTIES OF ACRYLONITRILE MONOMER

Molecular weight	53.06
Specific gravity at 20/20°C	0.8068
Boiling point at 760 mm Hg	77.1°C
at 50 mm Hg	9°C
at 10 mm Hg	—19°C
Vapor pressure at 20°C	83 mm Hg
Freezing point	—83.4°C
Solubility in water at 20°C	7.3% by wt
Solubility of water in at 20°C	3.2% by wt
Absolute viscosity at 20°C	0.4 cps.
Refractive index, n_D	1.3914
Heat of vaporization	265 Btu/lb
Average weight per gal at 20°C	6.7 lb
Flash point (Cleveland Open Cup)	45°F

A catalytic process is used to produce the lower acrylates. The starting materials are acetylene, alcohol and carbon monoxide. The catalyst is nickel carbonyl and hydrochloric acid. Union Carbide uses ethylene as the raw material and claims a purer product because of the absence of propionates.

The synthesis of acrylonitrile can be effected in two ways. The first is the dehydration of ethylene cyanohydrin into acrylonitrile and water in the presence of a catalyst under the proper conditions. The second method is by the reaction of acetylene and HCN at high temperature in the presence of a catalyst:

1. $OH—CH_2—CH_2—CN \xrightarrow{\text{catalyst}} CH_2{=}CH—CN + H_2O$

2. $C_2H_2 + HCN \xrightarrow[\text{catalyst}]{400\text{-}500°C} CH_2{=}CH—CN$

Acrylic acid and methacrylic acid can be made by variations of the methods already outlined, but they are generally prepared by the hydrolysis of acrylonitrile and methacrylonitrile:

$$CH_2{=}CH{-}CN + H_2O \xrightarrow{\text{H+}} CH_2{=}CH\text{-}COOH + NH_3$$

Acrylamide and methacrylamide are prepared in the same way starting with nitrile, but the conditions of the reaction are varied:

$$CH_2{=}CH{-}CN + H_2O \xrightarrow[100°C]{54\tfrac{1}{2}\% \ H_2SO_4} CH_2{=}CH{-}CONH_2$$

Acrolein or acrylic aldehyde is prepared by oxidation of propene at 400°C with an acid catalyst.

The substituted acrylic and methacrylic compounds are usually made by starting with the nitrile. As an example, α-chloracrylic esters can be made by reacting acrylonitrile with chlorine, the desired alcohol, and water, in the presence of sulfuric acid. The product of this reaction is treated with alkali and the α-chloracrylic ester is formed.

It should be noted that many of the manufacturing processes for acrylics use high temperatures and pressures and large volumes of cyanides. The end products are highly inflammable and potentially explosive. The lower molecular weight acrylates are also more or less toxic and have unpleasant odors. Some, such as acrolein are high-powered lachrymators. Acrylonitrile is quite toxic and irritating even by skin absorption. These factors add up to the need for extreme caution in the handling of these materials. It also means that their manufacture must be done in closed systems with carefully designed and maintained equipment, which is in turn reflected in the costs.

CHEMICAL REACTIONS OF THE
ACRYLIC MONOMERS

All acrylics are characterized by the fact that they have two reactive groups, either or both of which can react quite readily with other materials to produce useful end products. The end group, which may be a carboxyl, nitrile, ester, aldehyde, halogen, etc., is the first of these reactive groups, and the double bond between the first two carbons is the other.

Reaction of the end group is used for the making of higher-alcohol substituent acrylics. An example is the synthesis of cyclohexyl methacrylate. This is done by reacting cyclohexanol with methyl methacrylate, in the presence of toluene-sulfonic acid and a polymerization inhibitor. Acrylic esters reacted with dienes form cycloaliphatic esters according to the Diels-Alder reaction. Reaction of acrylic esters with acid yields propionates. Cyanoethylation with acrylonitrile has been used to produce useful products. The cyanoethylation of cotton fibers has been suggested as a means of producing a highly improved textile material that is mildew-, heat- and acid-resistant. Acrolein is indicated as a useful material to react with phenol, urea, etc. to form condensation-type resins or as a partial substitute for formaldehyde to produce modified phenolic resins.

The few reactions listed above are just to give some small idea of the scope of possible reactions using acrylics as chemical intermediates. An extensive body of literature is available that goes into discussion of these reactions in detail. Publications by producers of monomers cover the subject and are liberally referenced to primary sources.

POLYMERIZATION CHEMISTRY

The special reaction of the double bond in which the monomer combines with itself through this double bond is known as polymerization. The polymer has the same percentage composition as the monomer but a higher molecular weight. The molecular weight of methyl methacrylate is 100.11. Methyl methacrylate polymer in the form of cast sheet may have a molecular weight as high as one half million. However, the proportions of C, H, and O in both cases are identical.

Under various conditions of polymerization the end product may be of "low" or of "high" molecular weight. These are arbitrary terms that are used to describe polymer products, and as a generalization we can say that the lower the molecular weight the softer the material and the higher the molecular weight the tougher the material. The acrylic ester polymers can range from oily liquids to rigid solids, the differences being only the degree of polymerization, and whether they are of high or low average molecular weight.

The physical nature of the polymer is dependent on the monomer or combination of monomers used. In general, the lower acrylic esters are softer materials, ranging from the very soft and tacky 2-ethyl-hexyl and *n*-butyl acrylate to the tough but quite flexible methyl acrylate. The methacrylic esters are somewhat harder and esters of higher homologs range all the way to amorphous waxy polymers.

When the polymer formed consists of a straight chain of molecules characteristic of the acrylates it is thermoplastic: it may be formed again and again by heating to the point where it softens. The addition of varying amounts of crosslinking agents during polymerization that will form random bridges from chain to chain causes the polymer to become less thermoplastic and more thermosetting. In some cases a small amount of crosslinking agent will add desirable properties to the polymer and still leave it thermoplastic enough to form. Crosslinking agents are di-functional materials, such as dimethacrylates and diallylic compounds, and many others. Partially crosslinked polymers are used if better heat resistance is desirable.

If it is desired to shorten the length of the polymer chain, this can be done by the addition of small amounts of chain transfer agents. Mercaptans are generally used for this purpose because they are efficient and inexpensive. Chain transfer agents serve both to decrease the molecular weight and to narrow the range and variation of the molecular weights.

Most lower acrylic monomers will polymerize spontaneously at normal temperatures. It is therefore necessary that for storage and shipment these materials be inhibited. The inhibitor commonly used is hydroquinone or the methyl ether of hydroquinone in amounts ranging from 0.001 per cent to 0.10 per cent, depending on the activity of the monomer. Before polymerizing it may be necessary to remove the inhibitor. This can be done by washing with alkali or distillation under reduced pressure. In many cases the inhibitor can be overcome by the use of higher temperature or more catalyst in the polymerization and the operation of removal can be avoided.

In order to start the polymerization it is necessary to add energy in some form to the monomer. Although it will eventually polymerize at room temperature, this is a very slow process and generally elevated temperatures are used. Light is also a source of energy that can be utilized for polymerization, and there are instances where the action of sunlight or ultraviolet can be used. More recently there has been work done in the field of polymerization and rubber vulcanization by means of newer types of energy such as the radiation energy of gamma rays.

Molecular oxygen has been studied for its effect on polymerization, and its inhibiting action is well known. In some cases it is possible to overcome this effect by use of more energy and more catalyst, but in many polymerizations it is necessary to remove the oxygen by using a completely filled cell, or by blanketing the monomer with an inert gas, such as nitrogen or carbon dioxide.

Polymerization by means of light or heat alone is not widely used. Most polymerizations are performed with the aid of a catalyst. These catalysts are of the free radical type, such as benzoyl peroxide, which is soluble in the monomer or a persulfate that is water-soluble. The azo type catalysts have come into use recently and have proved their value. Benzoin has been found to be an effective catalyst for light-activated polymerizations. The use of activators with the catalyst is of aid in speeding up polymerization and for this purpose reducing agents such as sodium bisulfite or ferrous salts are added in small amounts.

Once polymerization has been started it tends to continue, like a chain reaction, at an increasing rate because the temperature is increased by the evolution of heat. It is necessary to control this exotherm to prevent a runaway reaction. The heat of polymerization of methyl acrylate is 20,200 calories per mole and of methyl methacrylate it is 12,900 calories per mole. This high exotherm is a major consideration in all industrial methods used for polymerization.

TYPES OF POLYMERIZATION

The many methods of polymerization and the variations on these methods can be considered as falling into three main classifications. They are:

(1) Polymerization in bulk
(2) Polymerization in solution
(3) Polymerization in heterogeneous systems.

Bulk Polymerization

Bulk polymerization is polymerization of the monomer as is, without the addition of any diluent. This is the method used to make cast rods, sheets and tubes. Uninhibited monomer is used and a catalyst added that is soluble in the monomer, such as benzoyl peroxide or azoisobutyronitrile. This is first made into a prepolymer syrup in a vessel by heating long enough to polymerize about 10 per cent of the monomer, and then cooled. The syrup is then poured into a cell and this is placed in a water bath or oven and polymerization is completed at low temperatures to facilitate removal of exothermic heat. When the polymerization is almost complete and the reaction slows down, the temperature can be raised to almost the boiling point of the monomer and polymerization is completed. At atmospheric pressures, very careful control is necessary to get a flawless casting, and one dimension of the casting must be kept to a minimum. Casting of thicker cross sections is accomplished by polymerizing at high pressures in autoclaves. Higher temperatures can be used under pressure and the cycle can be shortened. Products of bulk polymerizations are high molecular weight materials and are rigid and fairly resistant to solvents.

Polymerization in Solution

Polymerization in homogeneous solution is carried out by adding the monomer to an organic solvent in which both the monomer and the polymer are soluble. Such solvents as ethyl acetate, toluene and acetone are used with acrylic esters. Catalysts also soluble in the system are used. Some of the catalysts used are benzoyl peroxide, lauryl peroxide and *t*-butyl peroxide. The reaction is usually carried out at the reflux temperature of the solvent-monomer mixture. The method is valuable where the product is to be used in solution as in lacquers and some adhesives. Solution polymerization also produces the most water-resistant films. Products are generally of a lower range of molecular weights. Some control over the molecular weight is possible by varying the amount of catalyst, ratio of solvent to monomer and reaction temperature. Less catalyst, lower temperature and less solvent will produce polymers of higher molecular weight. However, the solvent acts as a chain transfer agent and very high molecular weight products cannot be made by this method.

Heterogeneous Polymerization

Polymerization in heterogeneous systems may be considered as a large number of very small bulk polymerizations. The monomer is mixed with water in which it breaks up into many small monomer pockets or droplets. Because of their small size, the total surface area of these monomer droplets is enormous and the water in contact with this large surface acts as an efficient heat-transfer medium to remove the exothermic heat. This eliminates the problem so evident in bulk polymerization and yields polymers that are easily handled in production at a rapid rate.

Heterogeneous polymerization is of three main types:

(a) Emulsion polymerization
(b) Suspension polymerization
(c) Granular polymerization

Emulsion polymerization is carried out by dissolving in water an emulsifier and water-soluble catalyst. To this is added the monomer, which is dispersed by agitation, and the surfactant. The batch is then heated and polymerization takes place. The emulsifier in earlier emulsion work was soap or simple surface-active agents such as lauryl sulfate. With the rapid development in the field of surfactants, many different systems are used for this purpose. A number of anionic alkyl aryl sulfonates and sulfates yield excellent emulsions of very small particle size and high solid content at low viscosity. More recently non-ionic surfactant systems have been developed that yield emulsions that are very stable to the action of electrolytes. The catalyst is a water-soluble persulfate. The temperature, method of addition of the monomer, chain transfer agents, activators, etc., can be varied to yield many different types of emulsions.

A major key in the control of emulsion polymerization lies in the surfactant system, which must serve at the beginning as an excellent dispersant, in the middle of the polymerization as a protective material to prevent coagulation, and at the end of the process must suspend the solid polymer particles in the water medium so that a stable emulsion results. Emulsions are made that have particle sizes as low as .01 micron and as high as 5 microns.

Suspension polymerization is carried out in much the same manner and with the same type of equipment as emulsion polymerization. The monomer is added to water and agitated to break it up into droplets of a few millimeters in size. When polymerization has been partially completed, these droplets would be sticky and tend to coalesce. To overcome this tendency a small amount of a protective colloid is added to the batch. Polyvinyl alcohol, bentonite, sodium polyacrylate and other materials serve this purpose. Unlike emulsion polymerization, where polymerization takes place in the water phase, in suspension polymerization the action is entirely in the monomer phase. Therefore, the catalyst used is usually monomer-soluble benzoyl peroxide. When the polymerization is completed the charge is screened to remove the water and washed and dried. The product is in the form of small beads which are easily handled and processed.

Granulation polymerization is a modification in which the monomer is added to a comparatively small amount of water with only the addition of catalyst. This is heated in a heavy-duty sigma blade mixer which continually kneads the material during polymerization. The polymer obtained is in the form of fluffy, granular particles. As no salts or emulsifiers have been added, these granules are extremely pure and need only to be dried before use.

TYPES OF POLYMER CHAINS

Homopolymers

Homopolymers are polymers made from only one mono-mer. A particular homopolymer has a definite set of physical characteristics. One may be soft and tacky, as ethyl acrylate; another may be rigid, like methyl methacrylate. If an inter-

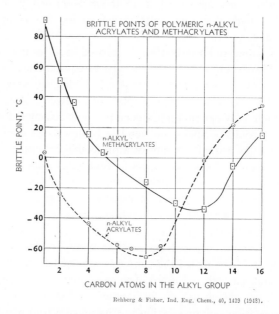

Rehberg & Fisher, Ind. Eng. Chem., 40, 1429 (1948).

The hardness and softness properties of acrylic and methacrylic poly-mers as a function of the alcohol substituent of the monomer.

mediate property is wanted, these two polymers, in perhaps the form of an emulsion, may be mechanically mixed. A film made from this mixture will be tough but flexible. It has been found that better properties are obtained by polymerizing the monomers together rather than mixing them mechanically. Almost all the acrylic resins used today are copolymers.

Copolymerization

From the molecular viewpoint a homopolymer is like a long string of identical beads. In a copolymer chain the string of beads would consist of two different kinds of beads strung together in a random pattern.

Copolymerization processes are identical with those of making homopolymers except for one major factor—different monomers polymerize at different rates. If we just mixed the monomers together without regard to this factor, and polymerized, we would get a progressively different copolymer composition as the polymerization progressed. Toward the end of the process we would have essentially a homopolymer of the slower-polymerizing monomer. A number of ways are used to get around this problem. Probably the simplest is to add the mixed monomers to the batch slowly so that each portion is polymerized before the next portion is added. Another way is to start the polymerization with monomers present in proportion to their rates of polymerization. Then add the remainder of the monomers in such proportion that the final product is of the composition desired. The monomer mixture that is added should join to the growing polymer chains and give a homogeneous product.

The literature covering copolymers is rather extensive, and it would be safe to say that every acrylic and methacrylic ester has been copolymerized in some proportion with every other member of the group. The products obtained are, in physical character, intermediate between those of the monomers used. Acrylic and methacrylic monomer esters have also been extensively copolymerized with other monomers. A complete list of these materials would run on for pages but a list of the most important ones follows:

vinyl chloride	butadienes and other dienes
vinyl acetate	acrylic and methacrylic acid
vinylidene chloride	styrene
vinylpyridine	acrylonitrile

In some of the above cases the acrylic ester is the major monomer, but the acrylate is often added in smaller proportion to improve the property of the other monomer.

In just the same way that copolymers add greatly to the list of available plastic qualities, so also tripolymers are found to be well justified in many cases. Frequently a resin shows excellent possibilities for a particular end use, but is deficient in just one particular physical characteristic. The addition of perhaps 1 or 2 per cent of a third monomer can serve to upgrade that property without disturbing others. An inexpensive third monomer may also be used to lower the cost of a resin.

In recent years, with the rapid growth of theoretical knowledge of copolymerization, two newer types have come to the fore. The first of these is *block* polymers. Referring once more to the "chain of beads" previously mentioned, note that this chain was stated to be a random arrangement of monomer units. Methods have been found to make the copolymer in a quite definite and repeating pattern of two different kinds of "beads." These are called block polymers and they display different properties from random copolymers, thereby opening up new possible fields. The other type is known as *graft* copolymers. Here a monomer is added to a polymer chain as smaller side chains. Both of these types and the techniques of producing them are quite new and have shown considerable promise. To make graft polymers it is necessary to reactivate the polymer chain to allow the new monomer to join with it, and acrylates have shown their value for this purpose.

3. CAST ACRYLICS: MANUFACTURE AND PROPERTIES

Of the wide variety of acrylic polymer resins, the best known to the layman are the cast methyl methacrylate sheets, rods, and tubes. Their brilliance and clarity are striking and quickly catch the eye. The unusual lighting effects possible by the use of back and edge lighting and the ease of formability have made their use widespread in such fields as advertising display, automotive parts, and other items constantly before the public eye. The almost gem-like quality of cast acrylic products and their resistance to aging have done much in the past to change the conception that plastics are a "cheap" substitute for the real thing. The present understanding is that plastics are new materials that can serve to enrich our civilization when used within their scope.

FACTORS IN BULK POLYMERIZATION

Cast acrylics are made by bulk polymerization, described in the preceding chapter. In its simplest form, bulk polymerization can be carried out by adding catalyst to methyl methacrylate monomer and then waiting for it to polymerize. If air is excluded and sufficient time allowed, the liquid will slowly harden into a polymer. Even without the catalyst, polymerization will proceed, but weeks or even months would be needed to achieve a reasonably hard product by this method. The liquid would slowly become more viscous, then become

33

a gel, and the gel would slowly harden into a casting. Even when a hard polymer finally resulted from the process, a portion of the monomer would be diffused throughout the casting and make it softer than desirable.

The effect of molecular oxygen on the rate of polymerization is well known. It has been shown to have a very definite inhibiting effect; hence bulk polymerization must be effected with all air excluded from contact with the monomer.

The catalysts used for bulk polymerization are organic peroxides that will dissolve in the monomer. Many of these peroxide-type free radical catalysts are available, but the most widely used is benzoyl peroxide. The more recently introduced free radical catalyst, α-α' azo diisobutyronitrile, has been growing in popularity. This is particularly true in colored sheets where the benzoyl peroxide has an undesirable bleaching action.

Polymerization of acrylic monomers is accompanied by the evolution of considerable amounts of heat. Unless this heat is able to diffuse from the polymerizing mass during the process, the temperature will rise rapidly and cause the monomer to boil. This in turn will cause a faulty casting full of bubbles and defects. Under certain conditions it is possible for polymerization to take place so rapidly as to approach explosive violence. At the beginning of the process, when the monomer is of low viscosity, heat transfer from the mass is a simple matter. When bulk polymerization reaches the viscous or gel stages, heat transfer is cut down very rapidly and the internal temperature rises abruptly. This in turn causes a more rapid polymerization and the evolution of so much more heat that the reaction may get out of control. The heat of polymerization of methacrylic acid esters is approximately 12 kcal/mole. This works out to about 55,000 calories evolved for every pound of methyl methacrylate polymerized. This heat evolution is further aggravated by the fact that polymerization does not take place at an even rate but builds up slowly to the gel stage, at which point it proceeds very rapidly, and then slows down as the residual monomer content decreases. About a quarter of the time of polymerization is accompanied by evolution of half of the total heat.

The specific gravity of methyl methacrylate monomer is 0.940. Typical cast methyl methacrylate sheet has a specific gravity of 1.19. This considerable difference is taken up by a shrinkage in volume during polymerization of 21 per cent. In evolving a practical method for industrial manufacture this factor presented many problems that had to be solved before flawless sheets were produced.

The raw materials for the manufacture of cast sheet are many. In all cases, methyl methacrylate monomer is the major ingredient. The catalysts are added in proportions varying from 0.01 to 1.0 per cent. Plasticizing of the sheet may be done by the addition of 3 or 4 per cent of a plasticizer such as dibutyl phthalate, or the use of a few per cent of a soft acrylic monomer such as butyl acrylate. The use of a small portion of methacrylic acid is helpful in preventing the sheet from separating from the glass cell prematurely. Stearic acid serves as a lubricant for easy separation of the finished sheet from the casting cell. Compatible pigments and dyes are added to make the wide variety of the colored, transparent, translucent and opaque sheets that are available. Special effects are obtained by using natural and artificial pearl essence, either with or without a tinting color. Ultraviolet absorbers such as salol or the newer proprietary absorbers are often used. Small proportions of various cross-linking agents such as CR39, other allylic compounds, and di-functional monomers may be used to increase the heat resistance, or eliminate crazing of the casting.

The methyl methacrylate monomer as received for casting is inhibited to stabilize it for shipping and storage. The inhibitor is hydroquinone in the amount of 1000 parts per million. To obtain the clearest casting and an easily reproducible process it is necessary to remove this inhibitor. This may be done by distillation under vacuum or by washing with caustic. A typical set of conditions for removal by distillation would be at 47°C under a vacuum of 110 mm Hg. A suggested washing procedure is to use 20 parts of a 5 per cent sodium hydroxide—20 per cent sodium chloride solution per 100 parts of monomer. This is followed by washing with water to remove traces of residual alkalinity. The uninhibited monomer must be used directly or if stored for a short time, refrigerated at a temperature not above 40°F.

The viscosity of methyl methacrylate monomer is very low —about 0.57 centipoises at 25°C. To use this, as is, in casting would present difficulties in leakage from cells. In order to overcome this problem the monomer, with or without catalyst, is heated to a prepolymer syrup. This serves also to remove dissolved oxygen that would cause bubbles in the casting, and to contract the mix so that shrinkage in the cell is minimum. A typical prepolymer syrup process would be to add about 0.5 per cent benzoyl peroxide to the monomer in an agitated kettle. This is heated to 90°C and polymerization is allowed to proceed to the point where the viscosity at 90°C reaches about one poise. The syrup is then cooled as rapidly as possible to room temperature and refrigerated until used.

THE CASTING CELL

The cell in which the bulk polymerization is carried out evolved as a result of the need to overcome all the aforementioned problems. It consists of two pieces of plate glass a little larger than the size of the finished casting. The two sheets of glass are separated by a flexible gasket and the entire mold is held together by clamps. The glass used for the finest sheet plastic is polished plate. Where the tolerances of the casting are not too rigid, tempered glass such as "Herculite" or "Tuf-flex" are used. Tempered glass is of value in minimizing the amount of breakage encountered in production. The glass must be spotlessly clean and free from imperfections and scratches because they will be transferred to the surface of the cast sheet.

The gasket is a tube of round or square cross-section made of a material such as plasticized polyvinyl chloride. The outside diameter and wall thickness of this tubing are chosen in such manner that it will seal the prepolymer syrup in the cell and will compress easily during polymerization and allow the glass plates to remain in contact with the polymerizing casting as it shrinks. The clamps holding the cell together are spring clips that will keep a continuous pressure on the cell all through the process. This will prevent leakage and will "take up" during shrinkage by compression of the gasket.

The cell is made up with one corner left open and placed on a surface tilted a few degrees from the horizontal. A carefully weighed amount of the prepolymer syrup is poured into the cell through the open corner and the cell is closed with the end of the gasket. The two ends of the gasket are butted together or lap-jointed to make a seal and more clamps added to put a little more pressure on the cell. Any air in the cell will rise to the somewhat higher filling corner. This air is removed by poking a tool between the gasket and the glass until all the air is removed and the cell is completely filled with liquid. The cell can now be returned to the horizontal position and, if carefully made up, there should be no leakage.

In the making of small sheets, all these operations are easily done by hand. The choice of gasket size, exact amount of prepolymer syrup of a standardized degree of polymerization, and even distribution of the spring clips will give a finished sheet with a close thickness tolerance. With larger sheet the cell becomes large, heavy, and correspondingly more difficult to handle. Bowing of the glass may occur with too much clamp pressure due to the hydrostatic pressure of the liquid in the cell, and thickness tolerances of the product will not be as close. Small cells use glass ¼ inch thick. Larger cells use correspondingly thicker sheets, and because they become excessively heavy, they must be handled by mechanical equipment. A number of filled cells are stacked on a truck with sufficient air space between them to allow for heat transfer. They are then ready for polymerization.

TIME AND TEMPERATURE

Polymerization of sheets of up to ½ inch thick is usually carried out in an oven under carefully controlled conditions of time and temperature. The air in the oven must circulate at a very high rate to assure the best possible heat transfer. The ratio of number of cells in the oven to the amount of air space must be kept as low as economically feasible to prevent overheating and consequent damage to the casting or the plate glass.

The ideal time-temperature cycle would be one in which heat is applied rapidly at the beginning of the cycle to the point where the exotherm becomes rapid, then cooling at a rate that would balance the exotherm, and finally heating to the highest point at the end of the cycle to complete polymerization. This ideal is far from attainable in practice. The danger of a runaway exotherm, boiling of the monomer, the economic factor involved in rapid cooling and heat shock to the glass cell all add up to the fact that, in practice, times of cycles are long and temperatures employed are low. For thin sheet of ⅛ inch or less the time factor is at least 12 hours and may be as high as 30 hours. Temperatures are in the neighborhood of 45°C for most of the time and are increased at the end to about 90°C to cure the sheet. Thicker sheets increase the time factor in geometric proportion and it can take as much as a week, in some cases, to complete the process. Thicker sheets will also use somewhat lower temperatures at the start of the cycle and during the height of the exotherm to facilitate removal of heat from the center of the thick cell.

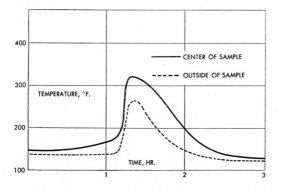

A curing-reaction curve for methyl methacrylate. The sample was a 2-inch diameter cylinder in a glass jar immersed in a water bath at 50°C. Most of the exotherm peak is well above the boiling point of the monomer and indicates why it is only possible to make cast items up to ½-inch thick at atmospheric pressures. (*Reproduced from Beattie, "Casting Plastic Sheets," Modern Plastics, July 1956.*)

The temperatures mentioned refer to the circulating air that is used both to heat at the start and cool during the height of the exotherm. It should be understood that the center of the cell is at a much higher temperature. If careful control is not exercised, this internal temperature may reach the boiling point of the monomer and result in defective sheets. Cooling with outside air may be required. After the height of the polymerization has passed, there still remains a small percentage of monomer that is diffused through the casting. This last few per cent is polymerized by increasing the temperature of the oven to 90 to 100°C for a few hours. Polymerization is then virtually complete.

The cells are then cooled to room temperature. The cooling process may be speeded up by the use of a fine cold-water spray. The shrinkage of the cast sheet by cooling will cause it to break loose from the glass plates, and, on removal of the spring clamps, the cast sheet and its gasket can be separated from the cell. The glass plates are then washed and stored for re-use.

For casting thicker than ¼ or ⅜ inch and up to about ½ inch, it is advisable to use a water bath for polymerization in place of the hot air oven. Better heat transfer through the water will allow for a shorter cycle and the use of somewhat higher temperatures in the process. After the exotherm has slowed it is desirable that the cells be transferred to an air oven to finish the polymerization at the higher temperatures required.

Cycles are frequently worked out so that the complete operation can be carried out in a 24-hour period, particularly in casting of thinner sheets. From the time the cells are put into the oven until removal of the finished product, there is no labor involved in an automatically controlled oven. The crew arriving in the morning can empty the oven, remove the castings, set up new cells, and refill the oven in a normal shift and then leave the polymerization to proceed until the next morning with a minimum of supervision.

CASTING PROCEDURE

A typical procedure for making a ⅛ inch sheet would be as follows:

(1) Wash methyl methacrylate monomer to remove the

inhibitor by agitating the monomer in a stainless vessel with 20 parts per hundred part of monomer of a solution of 5 per cent caustic and 20 per cent sodium chloride in water. The water-caustic layer, which has turned brown from the absorbed inhibitor, is allowed to separate and is drained off. This is followed by washing with water to remove traces of caustic. The uninhibited monomer is then dried over anhydrous sodium sulfate. The washing process results in the loss of 2-3 per cent of the monomer. If distillation were used this loss is reduced to about 1 per cent. The monomer is either used immediately or stored at 40°F in a refrigerator.

(2) A prepolymer syrup is made by catalyzing the washed monomer in a stainless, jacketed vessel with ½ per cent benzoyl peroxide. This is heated to 90°C for eight minutes, with agitation, then rapidly cooled to room temperature. Into the syrup is stirred 3 per cent of a plasticizer such as dibutyl phthalate and a small amount (less than 1 per cent) of ultraviolet absorber. Pigments, dyes and other additives may be also added at this point. It is then de-aerated by vacuum until a full vacuum causes no more bubbles to appear. The prepared syrup is then filtered through a cloth and stored under refrigeration or used at once.

(3) The cell is made up using ¼-inch thick glass and a PVC tube as a gasket. The cell is tilted, filled with syrup and sealed, bled to remove bubbles of air and returned to the horizontal.

(4) The cell is placed in the oven at 42°C for 14 hours, then raised to 97° in 1 hour and held at this temperature for ½ hour more. It is then cooled to room temperature and the cell opened and the finished sheet removed.

The process of casting in rigid cells causes all the shrinkage to take place in one direction only, as the glass sheets come closer together. This causes no problem as long as the polymerizing mass is fluid. When the polymer gel forms, this

Filled cells are stacked on cart shelves and wheeled into curing oven. The air inside the oven is circulated at high velocity to remove exothermic heat rapidly. (*Courtesy Modern Plastics, July 1956*)

Accurately weighed-out syrup is poured from stainless steel pitcher into tilted mold through a specially designed funnel. (*Courtesy Modern Plastics, July 1956*)

unidirectional shrinkage causes stresses to be set up in the sheet. After removing from the cell, these stresses would remain in the sheet and cause eventual crazing. If the sheet is to be heated to form a finished article these stresses would be relieved during the process. However, a goodly portion of the sheet sold is not heated, but machined to a finished product. To overcome this defect the sheet is annealed and the stresses relieved. The sheets are hung vertically in an oven and heated to about 140°C for a period of time depending on the thickness, and then slowly cooled.

To preserve the flawless surface of the sheets during handling, storage and shipment, they generally are covered with a masking sheet of paper held in place with a pressure-sensitive adhesive.

RODS, TUBES AND MASSIVE CASTINGS

When any dimension of a casting is less than about ½ inch, it is feasible to polymerize at atmospheric pressure. Should the least dimension required be more than this, it becomes impractical to manufacture in the normal way because removal of exothermic heat from the center of the polymer is difficult and boiling will occur, giving rise to bubbles in the finished product. Thick castings, up to any practical size, can be made by polymerizing in an autoclave at higher pressures. The higher pressure and attendant higher boiling point of monomer eliminate the problem of bubbles, and castings of considerable thickness can be made. Pressures in the autoclave may be as great as 100 psi and temperatures range from 40 to 135°C. A demonstration casting made in an autoclave was a perfect 16-inch cube with polished surfaces, and it had such brilliance and clarity that newsprint could easily be read through it.

Casting of rods can be done in aluminum tubes. A bank

of vertical aluminum tubes is filled with syrup and very slowly lowered into a water bath at about 40°C. Polymerization takes place in successive layers during the lowering of the tubes into the hot water. One process keeps a reservoir of syrup under pressure feeding into the tubes. As shrinkage takes place, more syrup takes up the voids created. The bank of aluminum tubes is then placed in an oven at higher temperatures for the final cure without any added syrup. The slight shrinkage at this point in the process is sufficient to allow easy removal of the finished rod from the tube. Rods of larger diameter may also be made in an autoclave. Rods up to 6 inches in diameter are normally stocked. Thinner rods up to about 1 inch in diameter are made, using a cell of nylon tubing. One end of the tube is tied and the tube filled with syrup. Then the other end is tied and the "sausage" hung in a water bath and polymerized. After curing, the nylon tube is stripped from the rod. The product is quite round and by the use of different diameters and wall thicknesses of nylon it is possible to hold the finished diameter of the rod fairly consistent.

Rods as produced do not have the high gloss and flawless surface of cast sheet. To get this surface it is necessary to machine and polish them on a centerless grinder. Cast rod of the larger diameters can also be manufactured by autoclave polymerization.

The casting of acrylic tubes is done by using a cell of aluminum tubing. A weighed amount of prepolymer syrup is poured into the aluminum tube, the air in the tube is replaced by purging with nitrogen or other inert gas. The tube is then sealed and placed horizontally in a device that will rotate the tube at a constant rate. The whole device is heated in a water bath or oven to polymerize. As the polymerization proceeds and the syrup becomes thicker, the polymer tends to form an even layer on the side of the rotating tube. By the time the polymer has reached the gel stage and will not flow, it has been formed into a tube of quite even wall thickness. The wall thickness can be varied by the addition of more or less syrup at the start of the operation. Shrinkage at the higher curing temperature allows for final removal of the cast tube from the aluminum tubing cell. The interior surface of the tube has a high gloss but the outer surface is mechanically polished. Tubes are available up to 24 inches in diameter and the wall thickness up to ½ inch.

SPECIALTY CASTINGS

Most of the cast sheet, rod, and tube produced is colorless and transparent, but castings are also available in a wide variety of colors. The addition of small amounts of compatible dyes in the prepolymer syrup makes for a transparent but brilliantly colored sheet. A variety of dyes and pigments used in varying quantities produce castings that range through various degrees of translucency to opaque products.

The incorporation of small amounts of artificial or natural pearl essence in the syrup yields cast sheet with various mottled and swirl patterns in a variety of colors. Orientation of the pearl essence is done in a variety of ways. Pattern may be obtained by photopolymerization through an opaque grid. In this method a small amount of benzoin is used as the photopolymerization catalyst; the grid is placed over the horizontal cell and it is exposed to ultraviolet light for long enough to come to a soft gel stage. Polymerization is more rapid where the grid is open to the light and the differences of contraction throughout the polymerizing mass orient the pearl in a pattern. The process is then finished in a water bath or air oven in the usual way. Another method is to incorporate in the cell a number of paper clips or glass beads. When the polymerization reaches a viscous stage, the metal clips are pulled through the viscous mass with a magnet or the cell is rocked back and forth and the glass beads disturb the mass. This creates the pearl pattern which remains and becomes fixed as the polymerization proceeds. Variations of the method of orienting and the amount of pearl essence and pigment create a large variety of patterns. Cast rod and tubes with an amount of pearl and pigment produce interesting beads and costume jewelry. The contracting force during polymerization orients the pearl and when the tube or rod is cut and shaped, interesting patterns result.

Cast products are also made by the use of a monomer-polymer slurry, instead of a prepolymer syrup. Acrylic ester polymers are soluble in their monomers and the incorporation of about 50 per cent of finely ground polymer in monomer results in a thick slurry. The particles of monomer will swell when the mixture is stirred and reach a stage where the mixture can be poured into a mold. The resulting casting is not of the high quality obtainable from syrup, but shrinkage is reduced and rapid polymerization is possible. The monomer-polymer slurry lends itself well to specialty products. Pearl sheets with interesting patterns may be made by incorporating ground particles of previously cast pearl sheet in monomer and polymerizing the slurry. The use of colored polymer particles in monomer gives interesting mottled sheets.

Specialty sheets can be made by starting entirely from scrap. Cast sheet cut offs, imperfect sheet, clean turnings, etc., are purchased by a number of companies and used to make monomer and monomer-polymer slurries. When this scrap is heated above 300°C it depolymerizes and yields a high percentage of monomer. This recovered monomer is somewhat yellow, and will not give high quality in clear castings, but for specialty sheet in color and pearl it is fully usable. At times, this monomer is available on the market at reduced price, but it is generally used for captive purposes.

DENTAL CASTINGS

An important use of monomer-polymer slurries is in the field of dental restorations. This is used in the making of dentures from the plaster mold in the dental laboratory and directly in the mouth, for fillings. For dentures, a polymer powder of fine particle size is mixed with monomer, catalyst and activator into a dough. This dough is pressed into the plaster mold coated with a release agent. Polymerization is accomplished at low temperature and short cycles. The use of small amounts of ethyl acrylate or ethyl methacrylate in the composition of the dough can control the flexibility of the finished denture. The use of a tertiary amine activator in conjunction with the catalyst permits the dough to set up rapidly at room temperature. This enables the dentist to use the process for fillings. The dough is mixed with a spatula, and pressed into the cleaned cavity. In about 5 minutes, it is completely set. Another few minutes and the filling can be polished.

Techniques for low temperature polymerization are improving rapidly. Many different types of catalysts and initiators, such as the di-acyl peroxides and the aliphatic azo compounds, have rapidly improved the art to the point where the largest portion of dental restorative work is done with acrylic compositions.

PROPERTIES OF CAST ACRYLICS
AND SPECIFICATIONS

Cast acrylic sheet, rod and tube are available in three grades. The general grade for most purposes is of good optical properties and is recommended for outdoor use. It weighs half as much as glass and has tenfold the impact resistance of glass. The heat-resistant grade has a higher service temperature than the general grade and is more resistant to crazing and the effect of solvents. The third grade is specifically to fit various military specifications as to optical clarity and lack of defects and is held to closer thickness tolerances. A table of physical properties appears on pp. 94, 95 and 96.

Cast sheet comes in a wide variety of sizes and thicknesses. Clear, transparent sheet is available from dealer stocks in thicknesses of from .060 to .500 inch in sizes from 3 by 4 feet and larger. The largest standard sheets are 6 by 6 feet and, in one case, as long as 102 inches. There is a large group of standard sheet sizes between the two extremes. Many sizes are obtainable up to 2 inches in thickness with finished surfaces and up to as thick as 4 inches in unfinished surface quality. Thickness tolerances vary with the size of the sheet and its thickness, but range from about plus or minus 12 to 20 per cent and higher in thinner sheets. Military specifications call for fairly rigid tolerances and it can be assumed that a fair portion of the sheet manufactured for military purposes, after inspection, is downgraded for general use because it falls below these tolerances.

Cast rods are supplied in random lengths and a range of diameters from $\frac{3}{8}$ inch to 6 inches. Cast tubes are made in lengths of over 4 feet and outside diameters from $1\frac{1}{2}$ to 24 inches. Wall thicknesses of $\frac{1}{8}$, $\frac{3}{16}$, $\frac{1}{4}$, $\frac{3}{8}$ and $\frac{1}{2}$ inch are standard.

A variety of standard colors are available in transparent, translucent, fluorescent and opaque for both indoor and outdoor use and custom colors are offered if ordered in certain minimum quantities.

IMPROVED CAST PRODUCTS

Cast acrylics have a number of inherent defects and much effort has been expended in an attempt to improve the hardness, heat resistance and scratch resistance of methacrylic ester castings. Generally, the improvements made have been accompanied by loss of other properties, such as formability and impact strength. Improvement in the craze resistance and solvent resistance has also been worked on, and a variety of cast sheets with improved properties are available. These sheets are generally expensive and their use is indicated in cases where the improvement of the properties outweighs the cost factor.

The use of allyl diglycol carbonate as a copolymer with methyl methacrylate has had a degree of success in the improvement of crazing and solvent resistance. The incorporation of over 10 per cent of the difunctional allylic compound causes a lowering of the heat resistance and at 20 per cent the heat distortion temperature drops from 90° to 70°C. In spite of this low heat resistance, copolymer sheets are used where crazing is a problem. The various other difunctional monomers have been tried as copolymerizers but have had very little commercial success. Among those that have been tried are various dimethacrylates, allylic monomers, phthalates and others.

Surface treatment has been tried as an approach to the problem of scratch resistance, and a number of post-casting surface treatments have been successful but costly.

One method of surface treatment involved the deposition of a cross-linked polymer on the surface of the sheet to improve scratch resistance. Another was to make a methyl methacrylate copolymer sheet with a portion of acrylic acid and then to treat it with a metal salt that would combine with the acid. Still another was the hardening of the surface of preformed sheets with an organic silicon compound.

A technically successful approach to the making of a superior cast sheet was the use of a halogen-substituted acrylate monomer. Polymethyl alpha-chloroacrylate sheet produced under the trade name "Gafite" has a higher heat distortion temperature, hardness, scratch resistance but still was a fully thermoplastic material and could easily be formed at elevated temperature. Unfortunately, the price was in the range of $20.00 per square foot and its sale has recently been discontinued. Work still goes on in the field of casting and perhaps an improved product at a reasonable price will be found to replace cast methyl methacrylate sheet.

4. FABRICATION AND APPLICATION OF CAST ACRYLICS

Acrylic cast products for fabrication are available direct from the manufacturers and from a widespread group of distributors throughout the country. Castings are available in sheet, rods, tubes, copolymer sheets, decorative sheets, massive castings, and specialty forms such as square and flat rods, and corrugated or embossed sheets.

TYPE AND SOURCES

By far the largest manufacturer is Rohm & Haas. Their cast products are confined to sheet stock, in a wide variety of sizes and thicknesses and colors and in opaque, translucent, transparent and fluorescent. The basic grades made are:

"Plexiglas" IIUVA (utraviolet-absorbing)

"Plexiglas" R: low cost sheet that has the same properties as IIUVA, but made to less exacting standards of optical and surface quality and thickness tolerance.

"Plexiglas" IAUVA: has lower heat and craze resistance than IIUVA, and is not recommended for outdoor use, but its lower solvent resistance makes it superior for application requiring solvent dyeing.

"Plexiglas" 55: is superior to IIUVA in resistance to crazing and has a somewhat higher heat distortion temperature. It is recommended for aircraft glazing.

"Plexiglas" 5009: flame-resistant sheet recommended for indoor architectural uses.

The major manufacturer of cast rods, tubes and massive castings is the Cadillac Plastic and Chemical Corporation of Detroit. This company began this portion of its business a few years ago when the E. I. DuPont Co. ceased operation of its cast products division. Cadillac is also a major distributor of cast sheet. Cast rod made by Cadillac is sold as "Cadco" HC-217 for general purpose and HC-218 for high heat resistance. General-purpose tube is HC-205 and heat-resistant tube is HC-206.

The Polycast Corporation of Stamford, Connecticut, makes cast acrylic sheet in sizes from 36 x 48 to 60 x 72 inches in both standard, heat-resistant and military grades and in thicknesses up to $\frac{1}{4}$ inch. These sheets may be transparent, ultraviolet-absorbing and ultraviolet-transmitting, and in a variety of standard colors. In addition, patterned sheets are available in pebble, hammered, diamond and ribbed designs. Polycast also has made copolymer sheets of acrylic and CR-39.

Cast Optics Corporation at Hackensack, N. J., makes standard acrylic sheet up to 48 x 72 inches and in thicknesses up to $\frac{1}{2}$ inch. These are available in translucent white and in satin finish. They also make a heat-resistant and military grade. Their CO-3 sheet is an acrylic-CR39 copolymer.

The Glasflex Co. of Sterling, N. J., manufactures specialty copolymer sheet, most for captive purposes. They also will make on order, various decorative sheets in pearl, color, surface treatments, etc.

Wasco Products, Inc., Cambridge, Mass., manufactures decorative sheets for architectural purposes. Their products are based on a technique of embedding various materials such as fabrics, leaves, etc. in the cell before casting. These "Acrylite" sheets are produced in color and various translucencies, and produce novel effects.

The Plastiglass Co. of Newark and the U.S. Plastics Co. in Metuchen, N. J., make a varied line of cast products from depolymerized scrap. Clear sheets made in this way are slightly off color and yellowed, but such specialty sheets as color and pearls are useful for decorative products. These sheets are somewhat lower in such properties as heat resistance and hardness.

Acrylic cast products are available from a large group of distributors located in many of our metropolitan areas. From these distributors, a buyer can obtain anything from a piece of sheet or rod to large quantities. Distributors in many cases are interested in doing a certain amount of fabrication of the simpler kind. They will cut sheets to size, machine rods to dimension, and polish them. They will do some simple forming and bending, and, in some cases, assemble parts. The following list is not all-inclusive, but gives some of the distributors and their location.

Ace Plastics	Jamaica, N. Y.
Aristocrat Plastics	Newark, N. J.
J. E. Barron	Cincinnati, O.
Transilwrap Co.	Philadelphia, Pa.
Plastic Process Co.	Los Angeles, Calif.
Plastron Specialties	Los Angeles, Calif.
Southern Plastics	Columbia, S. C.
Curry Arts	Scranton, Pa.
Midwest Plastic Prod.	Chicago, Ill.
Commercial Plastics	New York, N. Y.
Plastic Center	Newark, N. J.
Acme Plastics	Paterson, N. J.
Canadian Industries, Ltd.	Montreal, Canada

STORAGE AND HANDLING

For the protection of the fine surface of cast sheets during storage, shipping, and rough fabrication, the sheet is masked with a pressure-sensitive paper on one or both sides. It is important that the adhesive be easily removable and that it have no chemical effect on the acrylic surface. In those cases where surface scratching is not important, unmasked sheets at a lower cost would be used. The masking is lifted by one corner and pulled gently until the paper and adhesive are removed. Bits of adhesive that stick to the cast sheet can be removed by dabbing with the crumpled masking papers. Old sheets may present more difficulty in removal of the masking, and sometimes heating at 200 to 250°F for a brief period will facilitate removal. It is wise to store sheets away from sources of heat and sunlight, which will cause the masking to stick. It is also important to store away from locations that may be subjected to solvent fumes, which will damage the surface of the sheet and cause crazing and loss of brilliance. Storage of sheet for short periods in horizontal stacks is permissible if like sizes are stacked together without overhang; but for long storage the sheets should be stacked in racks in an almost vertical position.

The masking should be left on the sheet as long as possible during fabrication. All rough-cutting operations and edge-finishing should be done with the surfaces protected by the masking sheet. When it becomes necessary to remove this protection, extreme care in handling must be taken to prevent surface scratching. Sheets should never be slid one over the other and the area must be kept free of machining chips and grit. Slip-sheeting between operations is wise. For inter-mediate operations it is wise to take advantage of the pro-tective spray coatings that are available. These are sprayed on the surfaces, dry rapidly and afford excellent protection. When the protection is no longer required, the sprayed coat-ing can be removed as a film by lifting a corner and blowing with a jet of compressed air. The masking paper and sprayed protective coating must be removed before sheets are sub-jected to heating operation, such as forming or annealing.

CUTTING

Cast acrylics have machining characteristics that fall some-where between that of wood and soft metals. The woodworker who has had experience in the careful operation necessary for the production of cabinets in hard and brittle woods will find that acrylics present the same problems. The use of high-speed tools, carbide tips, and sharp cutters is necessary for clean work in both cases. Rigidly held work, prevention of vibration, and evenness of feed are important factors, as are the liberal use of jigs and fixtures and the avoidance, where possible, of hand work. In the same way that too slow a feed and the use of dull tools will burn hardwood, acrylic sheet will tend to heat up and then soften and smear. This results in poor cut surfaces and deviation from dimension. The use of care in both tooling and workmanship is "of the essence" in machining of acrylics, and it will show up clearly in the finished product because of the brilliance and optical proper-ties of the material itself.

For straight-line cutting of sheets to dimension the use of the circular saw gives good results. Certain precautions must be taken to produce cuts with the least amount of chipping. The machine itself should be of good quality and sturdily built with heavy arbor and bearings that will run true under full load conditions. The motor must be adequate to handle the load without stalling and to handle a 10 or 12-inch blade at 3500 rpm. A 1 h-p motor is minimum and 2 h-p is recom-mended. The blade should be a multi-tooth carbide-tipped blade corresponding to the mitre blades used in woodworking. Hollow ground or swaged tooth blades can be used where cutting is an intermittent operation. Blades should be gener-ally as thin as possible for cleanest cuts, but not so thin as to buckle and lose stiffness in operation. Sharpening of blades must be done by machine, or if done by hand, the blades must be run backward to stonedress so that no teeth are higher than others.

Multiple sawing is general practice particularly with thinner sheets. This can be safely accomplished if a traveling bed is used on the saw table and the sheets securely held on the fixture. The bottom sheet being cut should be backed with a clean plywood edge to prevent chipping. Chipping can also be held to a minimum if the blade is raised just above the top sheet as little as needed to assure cutting. Radial saws and traveling saws are useful for clean cuts to hold the product square and true.

A stream of compressed air at the cutting point will serve to clear away chips and keep the blade cool. A vacuum chip collector is useful to remove chips and preserve good house-keeping. For cutting of thick sheets, large diameter rods and tubes, a coolant may be needed to keep the work from over-heating and binding. Excessive pressure by the operator will result in poor cuts and dulled tools. The trick is to let the blade do the work; if it doesn't, remove it for sharpening.

The use of band saws is recommended for straight roughing cuts and for cutting curves. For straight cuts, a moving table and stop will allow cutting a number of sheets at once. A stream of air at the cutting point will keep the blade cool and remove the chips rapidly. Skip-tooth blades of hardened steel will give good rough cuts and allow for rapid feed. The wide gullet and spacing of the teeth will prevent heating and smearing. For curves, fine-tooth metal cutting blades are recommended. Feed is slower than with skip-tooth blades but the cut is finer and requires less finishing.

The larger the band saw, the longer the blade will last and the larger the piece that can be cut, but small saws are fully adequate for cutting smaller pieces. The usual care in adjusting the blade must be observed. Tensioning should not be overdone and too loose a blade will track poorly.

Guides should just clear the blade when it is running free. Under the best of conditions, a certain amount of chips, adhesive and masking paper will collect on the tires. If allowed to build up this will increase the blade tension and cause breakage and overheating. From time to time the tires should be brushed clean or solvent-washed to remove this material.

Straight cuts should use the widest blade the machine will take. Curves should use the widest blade that is compatible with the radius of the cut to be made. Inside cuts may also be made with the more expensive band saws that are equipped with a blade welder. Inside cuts may also be made with a jig saw. The nature of this tool is such that it is not satisfactory for production because just a few teeth do all the work and tend to heat up rapidly and give poor cuts. It is then necessary to back up the work often to remove chips and allow the blade to cool.

Inside holes are made with a drill press and a metal-cutting fly cutter. The work must be held rigidly in a fixture and the cutter guarded to prevent accidents. In order not to have to stop the machine between cuts, a knockout device operated from below the bed is useful. Very clean cuts can be made with a properly ground tool. The operation is rapid, and the cut is very clean. In most instances cuts of this kind require no finishing.

For the production of large numbers of strips or rectangles the use of rule dies is recommended for lower cutting costs. Except for very thin sheets, the stock must be reheated before cutting, and it is often necessary to reheat after cutting to square the edges and remove any markoff caused by the cutting operation. In many cases it is possible to form the heated piece and die-cut to size at the same time. The usual arbor press is used to provide the cutting force and the cast sheet is backed by hardboard or similar material to prevent damage to the cutting edge. It is also desirable in some cases to cut only partly through the plastic sheet, leaving all the small parts still in sheet form for subsequent operations. The press is equipped for this purpose with stops that allow the knives to penetrate just so deep into the sheets, and leave a few thousandths of an inch of stock uncut. After the subsequent operations, the pieces may be easily broken apart by hand.

MACHINING

Machining of cast sheet, rod, and tube can be done with the same machines that would be normally used for machining soft metals. The design of cutting tools is somewhat different from that of tools for metal cutting. Tools must be sharp and cleanly ground, but should have no rake and should give a scraping rather than a cutting action. This will give a clean, smooth and semi-matte finish that will require a minimum of polishing to bring out the best optical finish. Speeds and feeds are best defined by the experience of the machinist. It must be remembered that frictional overheating must be kept at a minimum to prevent gumming and rough cuts. Heavier cuts will require the use of water or soluble oil as a coolant.

Cutting to close tolerances can be done, but special care must be taken. Cast acrylic has a much higher linear coefficient of expansion than metals, and temperatures at the point of cut make a considerable difference in the accuracy of machining. A 10-inch piece of cast acrylic will change as much as 13 thousandths of an inch if machined at 90°F and measured at 60°F. It is wise, where close tolerances are to be held, to rough-machine and anneal and then to finish with a very light cut to dimension.

The use of tool steel is satisfactory for intermittent operation, but carbide will give better results in production. In some production turning operations even the use of diamond tools is well worth the cost involved. Careful arrangement of feed and speed and the use of diamond tools with a scraping action will give turnings a finish that is very close to a polish and no subsequent operation may be needed.

The most versatile tools for the machining of cast acrylic sheet are routers and shapers. The action of these two tools is essentially the same. A router is a portable tool that is moved around a stationary piece of work, and the shaper is a stationary tool used by moving the work against the cutter. The router can also be arranged in a stationary manner, in which case it is essentially a small shaper. In both machines the action of cutting is done by a small radius, multi-flute cutter running at high speed. Speeds of either may run as high as 25,000 rpm for very small cutters and rarely run at lower than 10,000 rpm. A minimum of two flutes is used for cutters that are adjustable and replaceable, and three to six flutes are used for fixed cutters. This high-speed, multi-cutter operation results in clean, almost polished cuts, and close tolerances.

Typical operations for these machines are finish-cutting of rabbeted and flat edges, nosed or eased edges, hole cutting of both round and odd shapes, rabbeting or carving of surfaces, blind hole cutting and a multitude of miscellaneous cuts that experience will dictate. Jigs and fixtures are especially useful in machining with routers and shapers, and it is well worth the time of the fabricator to refer to woodworking texts on the use of these machines with an eye to adapting the procedure to the machining of cast sheet. Once again the use of carbide cutters is advisable because the higher cost is justified by the quality of the finish obtained.

The drill press and the usual twist drill will easily cut holes in cast products. Again, small changes in the tool and technique will give better results. In thin stock, it is necessary to feed slowly to prevent radial cracking and the rake angle of the twist drill should be such as to scrape instead of cutting. Chip removal for shallow holes is not a problem, but for deeper holes it is necessary to use compressed air, coolants, and a slow feed to get best results and least distortion. Backing the cut with wood will prevent drill breakthrough at the end of the cut. The use of pilot holes close to dimension and finish cuts with a larger drill will produce better results than a single cut. The lubrication of the pilot hole with wax will give the finished hole a polished appearance which may be desirable.

Tapping and threading is done with standard tapping tools for nonferrous metals, but the tools are modified by easing the edges of the tool so that rounded grooves are produced. This will be pleasanter to the eye than sharp V-grooves and will avoid the possibility of cracks. The use of wax will give a polished appearance to the cut, and the lubricating action will aid in expelling chips.

FORMING

The thermoplasticity of cast acrylic allows it to be formed into innumerable three-dimensional shapes. When the material is heated beyond a certain point it becomes soft and pliable and can be folded or curved or stretched to conform to some predetermined shape. The simplest of molds are needed for this operation. When no stretching is involved it is not even necessary to use any pressure. The hot plastic is simply draped over the form and allowed to cool. Stretching is done by means of matched molds of wood or other easily shaped material, or by a single mold and gentle pressure such as compressed air or vacuum.

Certain basic precautions are necessary to get a good product. Pieces that by their nature would have to show good optical properties must be so handled while hot as to prevent excessive mark-off or surface defects caused by pressure against a mold surface or rough handling. The heating of the blank must be uniform and high enough to make the

Clamped ring jigs are used to blow cast sheet into many useful shapes. This dome will be cut in two, metallized, and used as a highway lighting reflector. (*Reproduced from the article, "For Highway Lighting," The Rohm & Haas Reporter, 16, #1, January 1958.*)

sheet pliable. Excessive heating should be avoided to prevent degrading the material. After the heating cycle, it is extremely important to form the piece rapidly before the temperature falls too low, for this will set up excessive strain that will cause poor shaping and crazing of the surface. The formed part must be cooled slowly and evenly in the mold and not removed until the cooling has been sufficient to prevent distortion of the finished shape.

The heating of cast sheet for bending and forming may be done by using hot air, hot oil, or infrared as a heating medium. The most versatile method is an electrically heated air oven. The sheets are suspended in the hot oven and the air circulated by fans. The heating elements are a series of strip heaters of high enough capacity to bring the air to temperature rapidly. The opening of the oven door to put in the sheet and to remove it when heated will cause wide fluctuation of the oven temperature, and the heaters must be able to compensate for this heat loss and hold a reasonable time cycle. Heating can also be done by gas heat. It is necessary to use a heat exchanger rather than flue gas to bring the air in the oven up to temperature. Large sheets may be clamped vertically in the oven and small pieces can be placed in felt-lined trays during heating.

Rapid heating of thinner stock can be done by an infrared heat source. This is a very high energy source of heat that will rapidly heat the surface of a sheet. However, the heat will not be conducted too rapidly to the center of the sheet and in thick stock the outside will become too hot before the interior is up to temperature. Sheets thicker than $\frac{1}{8}$ inch should not be heated by infrared. Sheets that are $\frac{1}{4}$ inch thick may use infrared if heated from both sides. Careful timing is essential when radiant heat is used and enough heaters must be used to cover the surface adequately. Although a very rapid method, it will produce poor finished products if not carefully controlled.

For the simple bending of a sheet or the forming of a portion of a sheet, it is possible to use spot heaters or strip heaters to bring just the portion of the stock to be formed up to temperature. Hot oil may be used as a heating medium for sheet plastic and will give excellent results. The oil temperature can be thermostatically controlled at exactly the temperature that the sheet is to be heated to, and heat will be the same at all points of the sheet. The time cycle in the bath will also control the evenness of the temperature throughout the thickness of the sheet. Of course, the hot oil clings to the sheet and it is difficult to handle and clean.

There is a range of temperatures used for forming and bending of a particular manufacturer's cast sheet. Within this range is an optimum figure for each type of forming. Too high a temperature will cause degradation of the sheet and too low a temperature will result in crazing and poor duplication of the final form. The manufacturers will provide charts showing a compilation of the best temperature conditions for forming various grades of sheet produced by them. Also available are the temperatures for different types of forming that may be used. Stock of other manufacturers may have other temperature optimums, and this should be checked before using. This is particularly true for copolymer sheets and partially thermosetting sheets which may require much higher forming temperatures.

Fabrication data charts (pp. 64 and 65) can save the fabricator many failures if carefully adhered to when establishing cycles and production schedules.

When the hot sheet is removed from the heating source it is necessary to work efficiently and rapidly to prevent the sheet from cooling before it is fully formed. Should the nature of the forming operation take an excessive amount of time, the results will be poor unless the mold is held at a high temperature. A preheated mold is helpful for large and highly stretched forms. Infrared lamps are a convenient way of keeping molds warm. A warm mold and a warm sheet will increase the cycle of the forming operation, but this may not

RECOMMENDED OVEN TEMPERATURE FOR FORMING "PLEXIGLAS"

| | Thickness of Sheet (Inches) | | | | | |
| Type of Forming | "PLEXIGLAS I-A" and "PLEXIGLAS 5009" | | | "PLEXIGLAS II," "PLEXIGLAS R," and "PLEXIGLAS 55" | | |
	.125	.250	.500	.125	.250	.500
Two dimensional (drape)	245°F	240°F	240°F	290°F	290°F	290°F
Air-pressure differential without form (free blown)	285°F	275°F	265°F	300°F	295°F	295°F
Stretch (dry mold cover)	285°F	275°F	265°F	320°F	300°F	300°F
Air-pressure differential with male form (snap back)	295°F	285°F	275°F	340°F	320°F	320°F
Grease forming						
Air-pressure differential with female form / Stretch with male form	320°F	300°F	285°F	340°F	340°F	340°F

MAXIMUM TIME AVAILABLE FOR FORMING "PLEXIGLAS" SHEETS IN STILL AIR BEFORE THEY COOL BELOW MINIMUM FORMING TEMPERATURE

Sheet Thickness	"Plexiglas" Sheet Temperature (°F)	"Plexiglas II," "Plexiglas 55" and "Plexiglas R" Formed in Still Air at Temperatures of		"Plexiglas I-A" and "Plexiglas 5009" Formed in Still Air at Temperatures of	
		75°F	120°F	75°F	120°F
.060"	360	0.5	1.3	0.9	2.3
.060"	320	0.4	0.6	0.8	1.2
.060"	285	0.1	0.3	0.5	0.8
.125"	360	0.8	1.5	2.0	3.5
.125"	320	0.5	1.0	1.5	2.8
.125"	285	0.1	0.3	0.8	2.1
.250"	360	1.5	4.0	4.0	6.5
.250"	320	0.6	1.5	2.9	5.0
.250"	285	0.1	0.3	1.5	3.2
.500"	360	2.5	6.5	7.0	13.0
.500"	320	1.3	2.0	5.0	10.3
.500"	285	0.2	0.5	2.5	8.0

Maximum Available Forming Time (Minutes)

be avoidable. Compressed air cooling is employed to advantage to speed up the cycle.

After forming, it is necessary to cool the piece slowly while it is held in the mold, particularly in thick pieces. It is even desirable to insulate against too rapid cooling that would set up high internal stresses in the product. Most important of all, it is necessary to establish a definite heating, forming, and cooling cycle that can be repeated on a production basis in order to get a reproducible finished product. When work is held up by lunch, coffee breaks, etc. it may be necessary to go through the cycle a few times to establish equilibrium again, and for large and critical pieces it is desirable to stagger the labor and continue the cycle without interruption throughout the working day.

For simple bending or twisting of the sheet the thickness of the sheet will remain about the same at the bending line; but in the case of stretch-forming, a wide variation of thickness will result. The deepest part of the draw will have the thinnest cross-section, and this will gradually become thicker as we go up the sides of the drawn piece. It is necessary to start with a thicker piece of stock for stretched work so that the thinnest portion still has the required thickness for good impact resistance. It is also worth noting at this point that in the deep-drawing of cast sheet with the attendant change in thickness, transparent colored stock will also vary in depth of color in proportion. If this change in thickness is gradual, the change in color will be gradual and may even enhance the beauty of the product. Conversely, if the thickness change is uneven, the color will be seen in uneven rings.

The shrinkage factor must be considered in the making of molds and forms for cast acrylic sheet. Depending on the sheet used, a good general rule is to allow for $\frac{1}{2}$ to $\frac{3}{4}$ of a per cent shinkage on cooling. If the sheet used is not annealed before purchase, shrinkage will be higher.

Forms and molds used in the fabrication of cast sheet can usually be made of easily workable, inexpensive materials. Wood or plaster can be used satisfactorily. The wood should be of a soft, fine grain variety and thoroughly dried before shaping. The plaster recommended is the high strength type, such as "Hydrocal," and should be reinforced with steel mesh, burlap, fiber-glass, etc. The finished form is covered with a soft fabric such as flannel, felt or velvet in order to minimize mark-off. The use of a variety of C-clamps or quick acting toggle clamps with or without clamping rings will firmly hold portions of a mold together or hold the sheet on the mold.

The surface of the mold must be well finished and free from waves or other imperfections that will show up because of the optical properties of the product. Specific patterns on the mold surface can be transferred easily to the finished piece and can serve to improve appearance where desired.

METHODS OF FORMING

When heated to the correct forming temperature the sheet of cast acrylic resembles a sheet of gum rubber. The application of moderate amounts of pressure will easily form it to the required shape. This pressure can be brought to bear by the use of a male and female die; air pressure or vacuum and a male or female single die; or with an air pressure differential without any die.

Forming of bends along straight lines is done by using a strip heater. The sheet is placed over the heater so that the line of the bend is heated. When it has reached the forming temperature it is placed in a simple jig that is able to hold it at the angle to be formed, and then allowed to cool. More than one bend in a sheet may be made at the same time by the use of a number of heaters correctly spaced and a multiple jig.

Forming of a sheet into a two dimensional curve is done with a single male mold covered with a soft fabric and a pair of strip clamps placed at the ends of the curve. The sheet

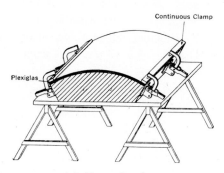

(a) Drape forming

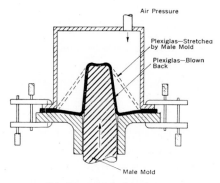

(b) Blow back forming

Four methods of forming heated cast sheets into two and three dimensional shapes. More complex shapes are best made with matched steel molds. (*Reproduced from "Four Dimensional Design, Fabrication, and Molding Data," The Rohm & Haas Reporter.*)

is heated to forming temperature and draped over the mold. The ends of the sheet are clamped with the strip clamps to prevent curling and the sheet is allowed to cool.

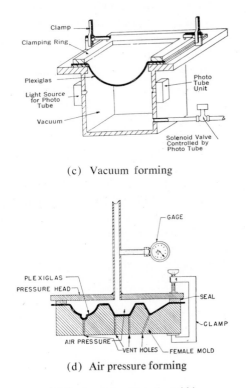

(c) Vacuum forming

(d) Air pressure forming

Methods of forming (cont'd.)

The use of air pressure differential as a means of stretch forming can make a surprising number of finished forms for the simple dies that are needed. The simplest description of this type of forming would be to call it intelligent bubble blowing. The particular advantage of this type of free-forming is that the piece does not come in contact with any part of the die. As a result, it has no mark-off and has excellent optical properties. Either vacuum or air pressure can be used. Vacuum is easier to use and to control, but vacuum can give a maximum differential of only about 14 pounds and if more than this is required to do the forming it is necessary to use air pressure.

The use of air pressure differential as a method of forming is confined to surface tension shapes. If other forms of a compound nature are required it is necessary to use other methods. The simplest of these other methods is the use of vacuum snapback forming. Advantage is taken of the tendency of the sheet that is vacuum formed to snap back to its original shape if the vacuum is removed while the sheet is still hot. The form is first drawn with vacuum and then a male die is lowered into the form. This die is somewhat different from the vacuum-formed shape. The vacuum is then removed and the hot part forms further by snapping back to the shape of the male die. Use of a greased male die will prevent mark-off of the product and make for good optical properties.

Vacuum snapback forming is confined to simple variations from the surface tension shape and cannot be used for complex shapes or sharp contours. For this it is necessary to have a female mold into which the sheet is forced by vacuum or pressure. Greasing of the female mold is necessary and vent holes in the mold are needed at all points where the sheet reaches the mold last, that is, the points of deepest draw. This method will pick up considerable detail from the mold and even surface patterns can be reproduced, if sufficient pressure differential is used.

Other methods of forming are variations of the methods described and may incorporate combinations of more than one basic method. Stretching of sheets is used instead of the simpler draping. The stretching may be done manually or by mechanical means. Plug and ring forming, slip forming, ridge forming, male and female mold forming are all used where the nature of the product requires it and the volume produced warrants a more elaborate setup. Experience will determine what method or combination of methods is best suited for a particular job and an understanding of the economics of the problems versus the quality required is acquired through trial and error.

PARTS ASSEMBLY

The assembly of formed or machined parts can be done by the use of many of the large variety of fasteners available. It must be kept in mind that the material is somewhat fragile and cannot be handled in the same way as metal or wood. Every drilled hole is a potential point at which cracking can start, and every fastener is a visually disturbing point in an otherwise optically pleasing product. Nevertheless, the use of soft metal rivets, grommets, threaded studs, and nuts and bolts are successfully applied and widely used.

Cements are preferred to fasteners for assembling, and if the cementing is done in accordance with established techniques and with reasonable care, the bond will be quite strong and of good appearance. The factors involved in a good cement joint are many, but the fit of the parts to be joined and the type of cement are of most importance. Surfaces that are well machined and without imperfections will joint well and give best results when cemented. Poorly jointed surfaces may appear to make good joints, but the stresses in the joint caused by making the pieces conform in the press may lead to eventual joint failure. The cement itself does not have the same strength as the cast piece. Heavy deposits of cement to make up for poor jointing will result in a weak bond.

There are two types of cement used; the first of these is the solvent type and the other is a polymerizable bonding material. Either of these or a combination of the two may be used, depending on the type of joint and the thermoplasticity of the material to be bonded.

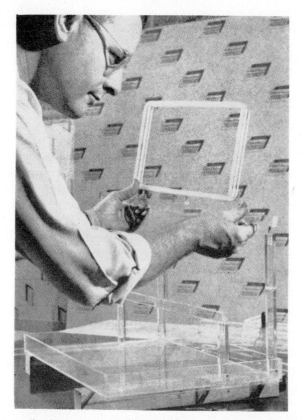

Cast acrylic sheet and rod being assembled as a display for jewelry. Simple cutting, one-dimensional draping, and assembling are used for merchandising displays. (*Courtesy of The Rohm & Haas Reporter, November-December 1952.*)

Cast acrylic sheet heated and bent to serve as a pedestal for double-tiered display tables. *Courtesy of The Bohm & Haas Reporter, November-December 1952.)*

For castings that are not cross-linked and are completely thermoplastic, the solvent cements will be adequate for indoor use. Solvents such as methylene chloride, ethylene chloride, and 1,1,2-trichloroethane are solvents suitable for cementing. Solvent cementing depends on the solvent soften-

ing the surfaces to be joined, so that there is a blending of
the two acrylic surfaces and the bond depends only on the
cohesion of the material itself. The solvent in time evaporates
completely and does not remain part of the bond.

In practice, one of the parts to be cemented is dipped or
soaked in the solvent. The surface in the solvent swells and
softens and the part is then brought into contact with the
piece it is to be joined with. After a period of time in contact
the soaked portion will mingle with the dry surface and then
pressure is applied to the joint and it is given time to dry
by solvent evaporation. To prevent blushing of the joint, it
is best to work in a warm room with low humidity. Only
gentle pressure is required to effect a bond, and excessive
pressure or distortion of the parts will cause crazing of the
surface. Even the vapor of the solvents can cause crazing
and adequate ventilation must be maintained.

The solvents used are of low viscosity and this may be
varied by the addition to the solvent of chips or shavings
of the cast acrylic. The chips will dissolve and make a
thick, syrupy material which can more easily be applied.
This syrup is still just a carrier for the solvent and the
principle is the same as for the soak method.

For joints that are to be used in outdoor applications the
use of the solvent method is not fully adequate and a cement
for this purpose is of different composition. A mixture of
about 60 per cent methylene chloride and 40 per cent
methyl methacrylate monomer is used. Before cementing,
catalyst is added to the solvent-methacrylate mixture. The
soak method is used to take up the cement and the pieces
are placed in jigs and cured at elevated temperature. High-
strength joints are produced by this means and good outdoor
weathering is obtained.

Partially cross-linked castings cannot be easily cemented
by the solvent method because the solvent will not readily

attack and swell the polymer. In this case it is necessary to polymerize a casting syrup in the joint to effect a bond. The partly polymerized casting syrup is mixed, just before use, with a peroxide catalyst and an accelerator. The catalyzed syrup is applied to the sanded joint with a brush or spreader and the parts assembled rapidly under light pressure. The cement will set rapidly and after about four hours will be ready for machining, although it will not reach full strength for a few days. Although not desirable, it is possible to form the piece after cementing if care is taken and only moderate draw is needed.

Various cements are also able to join cast acrylics to dissimilar materials. Various acrylic solution polymers are useful as cements in the joining of acrylics to glass, wood, rubber, metals and to other plastics. Each of these bonding operations involves special problems, and specific information from the supplier should be obtained to get satisfactory results.

FINISHING

All the machining operations that have been described leave surfaces or edges that vary from fairly rough to smooth, but in all cases there is a lack of polish of the machined part that is in sharp contrast to the perfectly polished surface of the original cast piece. If these surfaces are not hidden by the design of the object it is necessary to subject the machined face to a series of finishing operations to obtain the best possible polished surface. This is done by abrading the machined face with a series of grits ranging from coarse to very fine, in that order. The abrading operations may be divided for simplicity into three phases—sanding, buffing and polishing.

Sanding is done by hand or by machine and the very finest grit that will remove the worst imperfections is used. The use of wet-or-dry paper is recommended. This is paper that is waterproof and the grit is bonded to the paper with waterproof glue. The paper is soaked in water before use and kept wet during the sanding. The very same paper, if used dry, will leave a much coarser surface and many more superficial scratches that will be more difficult to remove in subsequent operations. The use of wet paper will also prevent a heat build-up in the sanding that may soften the plastic and cause smears and burns. Hand operation should always be done with the use of a sanding block to prevent excessive rounding and unevenness. Machine sanding operation is preferably done wet on such usual machines as belt and disc sanders. These sanding machines generally run at fairly high speeds for wood and metal, but for plastic sanding it is advisable to run them at slower speeds. In some cases it is possible to use dry sanding with finer grits with good results if the machine is of the oscillating type where the sanding paper is riding back and forth with respect to the piece being sanded and showing a new sanding surface continuously. The use of carefully constructed holding jigs and sturdy machines can hold sanding tolerances to a very few thousandths and will give surfaces that can be polished very rapidly to a fine finish.

The intermediate step in finishing is done by buffing. Cotton or flannel stitched buffs are used, and the abrasive medium is usually aluminum oxide in a grease binder. Cerium oxide is a newer material and gives excellent results, although it is more costly than alumina. The buffing wheel should run at about 1800 surface feet per minute and the buff should be wide and of large diameter for best results. The abrasive grit used should be chosen for the specific job; grits are available from coarse, fast-cutting to very fine grits that will leave a fair polish but cut slowly. It is of extreme importance to see that the various grits are never mixed. A different buffing wheel must be used for each grit and the part being finished should be cleaned after each buffing.

Ashing is a buffing operation in which a fast-cutting abrasive is used. The abrasive is usually a paste of pumice and water. Several grades of compound are used in succession and the operation is faster for production items than the use of sanding and subsequent buffing. The wheel can run at higher speed than in buffing because the water in the ashing compound has a cooling effect on the work. Ashing tends to round the abraded surface and does not give the clean, square effects produced by sanding and buffing. The rapidity of the operation will keep costs to a minimum.

Final polishing is done by use of a fast-moving polishing head made of chamois or flannel. If the previous buffing has reduced the scratches to a minimum, the polishing operation will result in a finish that is as good as the original cast surface. A coating of wax applied by hand will complete the operation. Sometimes the use of an oxy-hydrogen flame is made to "flame-polish" the part. This method requires a skilled operator who has had enough experience to just barely melt the surface to be polished without overheating and causing bubbles. Polishing by use of a solvent dip is sometimes used, but it is not desirable because it may result in crazing of the product.

ANNEALING

The finished product has been machined, heated and cooled irregularly in buffing, stressed in cementing, and subjected to solvents. All these treatments may result in rapid failure during use. To avoid this, it is desirable to subject the piece to an annealing operation. This will drive off any remaining solvent, finish polymerization of monomer polymer cements, relieve stresses, and give greater resistance to crazing.

Optimum times and temperatures for annealing have been worked out for varying materials and thicknesses. Annealing temperatures are kept as high as possible to shorten the cycle; but care must be taken, especially with formed parts, not to raise the temperature to the point where distortion will occur. After the heating phase of the annealing process the cooling must be done slowly and evenly to get the maximum benefit from the operation. The heavier the piece the longer the cooling should take.

PRODUCTS MADE FROM ACRYLIC CASTINGS

The clarity, chemical resistance, optical properties, formability, and weather resistance of cast acrylics have led to its use in a wide variety of end products. Many new uses are cropping up from day to day and a complete list of items using this plastic in whole or in part would cover many pages.

During World War II the use of acrylic sheet as an aircraft glazing material became established and the windshields and gunners blisters were all made of formed sheet. This is still used in commercial aircraft, but more modern usage in military aircraft has turned to laminated glass because of the high temperatures developed in jet planes. Commercial jets at present use triple glazing of acrylic sheet. The rapidly growing motor boat industry uses windshields and canopies of acrylic. Although the use of acrylic cast sheet to replace glass in windows is high in initial cost, many factories find that it is a good investment in the long run. This is particularly true where glass breakage due to vandalism becomes a factor.

Architects are specifying acrylics more and more often for many practical and decorative purposes. Integrally formed skylight domes have many advantages over the usual glass skylights. Breakage is negligible, and they remain airtight and rainproof—both common faults with glass skylights. The single formed acrylic part and a metal frame replaces all the costly and complicated sash and glass of the ordinary sky-

Trouble-free skylights for school and factory are one of the many architectural uses of cast and extruded sheets. They are formed from a single piece of clear or translucent sheet in many stock sizes. (*Courtesy of The Rohm & Haas Reporter, August 1959.*)

light and does a more efficient job for a longer time. A building that had been glazed with acrylic sheets was completely destroyed in a hurricane a few years ago but the glazing was undamaged. In areas prone to earthquakes, care is taken in the design of the buildings to make them resistant to shock, but glass breakage is expected. Acrylic glazing would eliminate this problem. A recently constructed office building used 12 foot long panels of acrylic sheet for outside sheathing. The non-transparent sheets were installed as curtain walls over plywood. Another exterior development of acrylic sheet is its use in louvered windows and doors of the jalousie type. The movement of the vanes of the jalousie and the optical properties of the acrylic serve to control the amount of daylight brought into the building.

Interior architectural uses include such items as room dividers, partition structures, shower enclosures and doors. For these interior uses many of the embossed and decorative sheets have been used to advantage. Gratings and diffusion shields on lighting fixtures are frequently of cast acrylic, as are the sheets used in hanging luminous ceilings so frequently used for general lighting in public buildings.

Probably the largest single use of acrylic sheet is in the rapidly growing outdoor sign business. The backgrounds and faces of signs are of flat or formed sheets and the cut out letters are of the same material. These signs are efficient both night and day, and the use of internal face lighting and backlighting of the lettering at night make for interesting and effective signs. Acrylics are used for counter dividers and window and counter display fixtures in stores. Very effective mannequins made of formed acrylic sheet are used for clothing display.

Many parts of juke boxes and dispensing machines are made of acrylic and the use of colored sheets and edge lighting make for spectacular and gaudy, if not very artistic products. Manufacturers of machinery use acrylic sheet for safety shields and inspection windows and acrylic housings and parts for demonstration items. Bilge pumps are manufactured of acrylic parts to overcome the deleterious action of sea water.

The medical profession has found numerous uses for acrylics for instruments used in examination and in orthopedic devices. The light piping property of acrylic rods is used in special instruments for internal examination. An external light source can be carried through curved acrylic rod directly to the anatomical portion to be observed. Orthopedic devices take advantage of the impact strength and light weight of the acrylic as well as the chemical inertness of the plastic. Hospitals use acrylics for many types of equipment such as baby bassinets of one piece acrylic moldings. One interesting use of acrylics is in the making of artificial eyes. Acrylic blanks are carefully finished by expert craftsmen to resemble the human eye in every detail. Contact lenses are being made of cast acrylics.

A common use of acrylic cast sheet in almost every home is the protective shield over the face of the television tube. Although glass is often used for this purpose, acrylic-formed implosion shields are considered safer and better. Automobile dashboard instruments are usually provided with acrylic faces. Edge lighting of these panels allows the instruments to be easily read without creating light glare in the driver's eyes.

The unbreakable watch crystal involved many plastic materials in the course of its development and was never a really satisfactory product until cast sheet of acrylic was used in its manufacture. At present, partially thermosetting copolymer cast acrylic sheet is used for this purpose almost exclusively. Faces of delicate instruments use acrylics in place of glass to eliminate the damage that could be caused by glass breakage. In the course of the last few years, more and more lenses are being made of acrylics. At first, this was confined to the inexpensive items, such as flashlight lenses or magnifying glasses, but as knowledge of the manufacturing problems has matured, the use of acrylic lenses is invading more and more of this traditionally glass-oriented field.

Instrument faces are being laminated in a hot press. The acrylic backing sheet will be edge-lighted in use and will allow the operator to read the instrument without glare. (*Courtesy of The Rohm & Haas Reporter,* **14,** *#2, March-April 1956.*)

This elaborate press operation is used for forming heat-softened acrylic cast sheet into the windshield of an airplane. (*Courtesy of The Rohm & Haas Reporter,* **14**, *#2, March-April 1956.*)

Last, but far from least, is the field of decorative home items. The number of acrylic cigarette boxes, jewel cases, napkin holders, and similar miscellaneous items made by the small factory and the home craftsman is beyond the possibility of inventorying. The general appeal of this plastic can easily be seen by looking over the gift counter at the department store and noting how many of the articles are made totally or in part with acrylics.

5. MOLDING POWDERS: THEIR MANUFACTURE AND USE

When the original work was being done in the development of bulk polymerization that resulted in acrylic cast sheet, rods and tubes, the possibility of using these bulk polymers for injection molding was immediately investigated. The bulk polymer was ground into small granules which were used as a molding powder. This work was done by Hill in England and a number of United States and British patents were issued covering this work.

The injection moldings obtained revealed a number of problems that had to be worked out. A good molding material should be of fairly high molecular weight to get a tough, hard-surfaced molding. It should also have good flow characteristics so that it fills the mold easily and should have minimum shrinkage and distortion when cooled and used. The moldings made by bulk polymer granules did not fit these characteristics very well. The molecular size of bulk polymers covers quite a wide range. It has a small proportion of both low and very high molecular weight chains. This wide range and lack of homogeneity caused the material to have bad flow characteristics and the high weight portion imparted an elastic memory to the molding that caused undesirable distortion. The cost factor was also important, and the bulk polymer is costly to produce. The cost was still further increased by the necessity of grinding the bulk polymer into the uniform granules needed for the molding machine.

SUSPENSION POLYMERIZATION

Many attempts to improve the product were made, all of which avoided bulk polymer methods and aimed at polymerization in a liquid medium. The use of water and alcohol as the medium led to various spongy polymers that were easily broken into a powder. The use of water and various additives led to the beginnings of emulsion polymerization. Under specific conditions where emulsion did not take place but little droplets of monomer polymerized in suspension, these droplets were recoverable as beads of polymer. These beads, when washed and dried, proved to be a useful molding material.

From these first trials the art of suspension polymerization grew rapidly. Methods of controlling the bead size were developed as were ways of getting pure and uncontaminated beads. It was found that the washed and dried bead was further improved as a molding material by hot milling or extruding and then chopping to a uniform size. It appears that the shearing forces on the beads when milling or extruding tend to break down the high molecular weight portion into smaller chains and yield molding granules with a quite narrow range of molecular weight. This makes for a dimensionally stable product and sharper melting range in the molding machine.

Suspension polymerization is, in essence, a large number of bulk polymerizations of small droplets of monomer while they are suspended in a water medium. The catalyst used is an oil-soluble peroxide, usually benzoyl peroxide, and polymerization takes place entirely in the monomer droplets. The water suspension medium serves to keep the droplets separated and acts as a heat-transfer medium to carry off the heat of polymerization. Because of the efficiency of heat transfer through the water, the temperature of the bath remains constant and, unlike bulk polymerization, it is possible to get rapid conversion to polymer in comparatively short cycles.

The main problem in suspension polymerization is to obtain a uniform monomer droplet of the desired size and to hold this droplet in suspension for the entire cycle. The droplet is produced by the agitation of the mass. The speed, type of agitator, and shape and size of the vessel are of greatest importance. Any change in one of these factors will change the size of the droplet and the resulting polymer. In practice, it is necessary to work out these factors for the given piece of production equipment and to adhere strictly to the established method to get a reproducible product.

To maintain these droplets and to prevent agglomeration of the partially polymerized monomers it is necessary to add a suspension agent or a protective colloid. Finely powdered materials that have been used for this purpose include talc, kaolin, magnesium carbonate, barium sulfate, and aluminum oxide. Protective colloids used include polyvinyl alcohol, soluble starch, gelatin, glycol cellulose and sodium polymethacrylate.

The other factors involved in the suspension polymerization are pH control, accomplished by use of a buffer system, and careful control of the temperature of reaction, on which the molecular weight of the beads depends.

A method that has been used commercially for the production of beads is as follows:

> 1 part methyl methylacrylate
> 2 parts water
> 8 to 18 grams per liter of magnesium carbonate
> 0.2% benzoyl peroxide catalyst.

For the production of large beads, 8 to 10 grams of magnesium carbonate is used per liter; for fine granules, 18 grams per liter is used. The reaction is stirred and heated to

80°C. The heat of reaction drives the temperature to 120°C and the internal pressure rises to 3½ atmospheres. The agitator is driven at a speed of 130 rpm. The agitator is designed to perform its task without the formation of any pockets in the liquid. Too slow a stirrer speed gives large granules which may cohere in clumps.

Polymerization is complete in about one hour. The vessel is cooled and sulfuric acid is added. The acid dissolves the magnesium carbonate from the surface of the beads of polymer. The beads are separated from the water phase by filtering through a screen and are than washed five times with water to assure removal of all trace of sulfuric acid. They are finally dried in aluminum trays at a depth of about 1 inch at 80°C for 8 hours. The yield of pearls of less than 1 mm in diameter is greater than 97 per cent.

Other methods published have used a small proportion of an emulsifier such as "Aerosol OT" and sodium lauryl sulfate. These emulsifiers help to control particle size and keep the beads in suspension. Emulsification is to be avoided. For economical suspension polymerization the ratio of monomer to water should be high and the cycle as short as possible. To obtain best results, regulating agents are often used. Very small amounts of trichloroethylene and lauryl mercaptan serve this purpose. At the tacky stage the addition of a lubricant such as stearic acid helps to prevent agglomeration. The final operation is to mill the beads on hot mixing rolls with additives such as colorants and to grind the milled product into a finished molding powder. It is also possible to dissolve the beads into a solvent such as toluene, xylene or butyl acetate for use as a lacquer.

Recent work by the Eastern Regional Laboratory of the Department of Agriculture has led to an interesting modification of suspension polymerization. In this process the monomer is polymerized in a heavy duty mixer with kneading type

Properties Chart of Acrylic Moldings Made from Three Grades of Du Pont "Lucite"

PROPERTY	UNITS	A.S.T.M. METHOD	"LUCITE" 40 and 140	"LUCITE" 29 and 129	"LUCITE" 30 and 130
Mechanical					
Tensile strength, 0.125 in. thick −70°F.	psi	D638−52T	14.5 x 10³	14.5 x 10³	14.5 x 10³
73°F.	psi	D638−52T	10.5 x 10³	10.0 x 10³	9.5 x 10³
158°F.	psi	D638−52T	>5.0 x 10³	>4.0 x 10³	>3.5 x 10³
Tensile elongation −70°F.	per cent	D638−52T	2	2	2
73°F.	per cent	D638−52T	3-5	3-5	3-5
158°F.	per cent	D638−52T	80	90	100
Tensile and flexural modulus of elasticity 73°F.	psi	D638−52T	4.5 x 10³	4.5 x 10³	3.5-4.5 x 10³
Shear strength	psi	D732−46	9.4 x 10³	9.0 x 10³	7.5 x 10³
Impact strength, Izod, milled notch, 0.250 in. bars 73°F.	ft.lb./in.	D256−54T	0.3	0.3	0.3
Stiffness 73°F.	psi	D747−50	4.3 x 10³	4.1 x 10³	3.4 x 10³
Flexural strength 73°F.	psi	D790−49T	1.6 x 10⁴	1.5 x 10⁴	1.5 x 10⁴
Hardness, Rockwell		D785−51	M103	M95	M88
Thermal					
Coefficient of linear thermal expansion (0-100°F., aver.) ⁽⁾	in./in./°F.	D696−44	3 x 10⁻⁵	4 x 10⁻⁵	4 x 10⁻⁵
Thermal conductivity	B.T.U. hr./sq.ft./°F./in	Cenco-Finch	1.4	1.4	1.4
Specific heat			0.35	0.35	0.35
Deformation under load, 2000 psi 24 hours, 122°F.	per cent	D621−51	0.3-0.4	0.7	0.35
Heat distortion temperature 264 psi	°F.	D648−45T	202	180	166
66 psi	°F.	D648−45T	216	190	175

Electrical

Property	Units	Test Method			
Dielectric strength[2], short time, 0.125 in.	v/mil	D149—55T	400	400	400
Arc resistance		D495—48T	No tracking	No tracking	No tracking
Volume resistivity	ohm-cm	D257—49T	$>10^{15}$	$>10^{14}$	$>10^{14}$
Dielectric constant 60 cycles		D150—47T	3.5	3.9	3.9
10^3 cycles		D150—47T	3.2	3.4	3.6
10^6 cycles		D150—47T	2.7	2.9	2.9
Dissipation factor 60 cycles		D150—47T	0.06	0.04	0.04
10^3 cycles		D150—47T	0.04	0.04	0.04
10^6 cycles		D150—47T	0.02	0.03	0.03

Optical

Property	Units	Test Method			
Index of refraction	n_D	D542—50	1.489-1.493	1.489-1.493	1.489-1.493
Dispersion	$(n_D-1)/(n_F-n_C)$		49	49	49
Luminous transmittance, 0.125 in.	per cent	D791—54	>92	>92	>92
Haze	per cent	D1003—52	<3	<3	<3

Miscellaneous

Property	Units	Test Method			
Water absorption, 24 hour					
Weight gain plus soluble matter loss	per cent	D570—54T	0.3	0.3	0.3
Soluble matter loss	per cent	D570—54T	<0.1	<0.1	<0.1
Flammability, 0.125 in.[3]	in./min.	D635—44	0.9-1.2	0.9-1.2	0.9-1.2
Specific gravity		D792—60	1.19	1.18	1.18
Mold shrinkage	in./in.		0.003-0.007	0.002-0.007	0.002-0.006
Odor			none	none	none
Taste			none	none	none

(1) Data shown are average values and should not be used for specifications.
(2) For 0.125 in. thick specimens. For 0.0625 in. thickness, values are approximately 50% higher.
(3) For 0.125 in. thick specimens. Thicker specimens give greatly reduced rates by this test.
(4) Apparent expansion is influenced as much by conditions under which specimen was prepared as by temperature change; hence, these values are useful only as guides.

Except for optical tests, all specimens were annealed under following conditions:

Annealing Temp.		Annealing Time	
L. 30 & 130	140°F.	⅛" thick	2 hrs.
L. 29 & 129	160°F.	¼" thick	4 hrs.
L. 40 & 140	180°F.		

agitator. A very small amount of water is used and some lubricant. The reaction is run at reflux using either an oil- or water-soluble catalyst. The kneading action causes formation of a granular polymer; hence the process is called granulation polymerization. It is claimed that the product is useful as a molding powder.

PROPERTIES OF MOLDING POWDERS

Methyl methacrylate molding powders available in the United States are produced by DuPont and Rohm & Haas. DuPont's "Lucite" is available in three grades determined by flow characteristics and heat resistance. Each of these grades have two variations, one of which is adapted for injection molding and the other for extrusion. Rohm & Haas' "Plexiglas" is produced in corresponding grades.

A comparison of products made of molding powder versus cast products shows that the cast acrylic is a better product. Cast sheet is harder than extruded sheet, has a higher tensile strength, lower elongation, better heat distortion properties and generally possesses better machining properties and a more optically perfect surface. Many improvements in manufacture have been made in extruded sheet in recent years, and healthy competition now exists between cast and extruded sheet and rod for the available market. At the present time, extruded sheets up to ⅛ inch thick have the price edge over cast sheet, while above this thickness the cast sheet is somewhat less expensive. Chemical, electrical and weathering properties compare favorably for both types of product. Extruded sheet is more difficult to handle at forming temperature, is softer than cast sheet and more likely to stick together if touched or folded. The cementing of extruded sheet is also more difficult, needs stronger cements and the soak method may not be used.

INJECTION MOLDING

The list of useful articles made by injection molding of acrylic molding powders is growing at a rapid rate. Many articles formerly made by the machining of cast acrylics are now being made at much lower cost by injection molding. This is particularly true of the more complex shapes that would need considerable labor for machining. Improvements in the molding art over the years and the improvements in molding powders now make for highly acceptable molded products.

Injection molding of acrylics is done on standard machines in much the same way that styrene and other plastics are handled. Injection molding ordinarily uses temperatures of 180 to 250°C and pressures from 10,000 to 35,000 psi. Compression molding can be carried out at lower temperatures and pressures, but this is used very little.

Acrylic moldings are preferred to other plastics in those cases where the superior optical properties and outdoor weatherability are factors. They also are indicated where high resistance to chemical action and dimensional stability are required. The gates, sprues and runners can be reground and used, but it is advisable that reground material be used on less critical parts and not mixed with virgin material. Reground material will pick up dirt and lint rapidly because of the static charge developed on grinding and it is almost impossible to keep it dust-free.

Despite careful packaging, the molding powder will have a small percentage of moisture. This tendency to absorb moisture is characteristic of the material, and predrying before molding is suggested as necessary to get consistently good moldings that are free from defects and to avoid the need to change molding conditions. Wet molding powder causes changes in the feed temperature into the mold, and this will affect the temperature and pressure conditions in the mold. Two to three hours of drying time in tray ovens or hopper

The production of acrylic lenses by injection molding has been growing at a rapid rate. Extreme care in mold making and in press cycling results in an excellent product. (*Courtesy of The Rohm & Haas Reporter, 15, #3, May-June 1957.*)

dryers are recommended at a temperature of 180 to 200°F to eliminate this problem.

Actual molding conditions are described in the table on pp. 94-96. It should be noted that the recommended temperatures and pressures cover a fairly wide range and the molding operation is not particularly critical as compared to a material such as nylon. Acrylics also show but little tendency to degrade during the molding, and higher ranges of temperature will still give a satisfactory product.

Particular care must be given to the problem of producing a stress-free molding insofar as possible. For this reason it is recommended that the shot weight be limited to no more than 75 per cent of the rated capacity of the machine and that the mold be heated. Articles that are to be decorated should be annealed after molding. Stresses remaining after molding will cause crazing when decorated if the molding is not annealed.

Shrinkage of acrylic moldings is a minor factor and is quite small when compared to other molding plastics. However, for such precise products as lenses and watch crystals, even this small shrinkage must be controlled by good molding cycles and constant temperatures. In some operations, special devices such as back pressure on sliding molds are used to hold shrinkage in two dimensions to virtually zero. It is also necessary in optical parts to use specially designed molds to eliminate the need for the usual knockout pins that would mar the molded surface.

The design of molds is of great importance, and multiple-cavity molds must be well balanced as to runner length, gates and venting. In acrylics, even more than in other plastics, the design of the mold is a specialized art and can be done well only by the experienced mold maker, who fully understands the high quality of product usually required of acrylic moldings. The prevention of sink marks, correct placement of the gate and runner, flow from thick to thin sections, and intelligent use of ribs and bosses to reduce the amount of material needed are all part of the designers and mold makers trade.

PROPERTIES OF CAST, MOLDED AND MODIFIED ACRYLICS *

PROPERTIES	A.S.T.M. TEST METHOD	ACRYLIC		Modified Acrylic Molding Compound
		Methyl Methacrylate		
		Cast	Molding	
Molding qualities	—	Good	Excellent	Excellent
Compression molding temp., °F	—		300-425	300-400
Compression molding pressure, psi	—		2000-10000	2000-5000
Injection molding temp., °F	—		325-500	400-490
Injection molding pressure, psi	—		10000-20000	10000-20000
Compression ratio	—		1.6-2.0 Compression	—
Mold shrinkage, in. per in.	—	—	0.001-0.004 injection 0.002-0.008	0.004-0.008
Specific gravity	D792	1.17-1.20	1.17-1.20	1.12-1.18
Specific volume, cu in. per lb	D792	23.7-23.1	23.7-23.1	24.7-23.3
Refractive index, n_D	D542	1.48-1.50	1.49	Not Applicable
Tensile strength, psi	D638, D651	8000-11000	7000-11000	5000-9000
Elongation, %	D638	2-7	3-10	>15-50
Modulus of elasticity in tension, 10^5 psi	D747	3.5-5.0	4.5	2.0-4.0
Compressive strength, psi	D695	11000-19000	12000-18000	2000-14000
Flexural strength, psi	D790	12000-17000	13000-17000	8000-13000

Property	ASTM			
Impact strength, ft.-lb. per in. of notch ($\frac{1}{2}$ x $\frac{1}{2}$ in. notched bar, Izod test)	D256	0.4-0.5	0.3-0.5	0.5-3.0
Hardness, Rockwell	D785	M80-M100	M85-M105	R-100-R-200
Thermal conductivity	C177	4-6	4-6	4-5
Specific heat, cal. per °C per gm	—	0.35	0.35	0.34
Thermal expansion, 10^{-5} per °C	D696	5-9	5-9	6-8
Resistance to heat, °F (continuous)	—	140-200	140-190	160-185
Heat distortion temp., °F	D648	150-210	160-195	170-190
Volume resistivity	D257	$>10^{15}$	$>10^{14}$	2.0×10^{16}
Dielectric strength	D149	450-550	450-550	400-500
Dielectric strength	D149	350-400	350-400	400-500
Dielectric constant, 60 cycles	D150	3.5-4.5	3.5-4.5	3.0-4.0
Dielectric constant, 10^3 cycles	D150	3.0-3.5	3.0-3.5	2.5-3.5
Dielectric constant, 10^6 cycles	D150	2.2-3.2	2.2-3.2	2.0-3.0
Dissipation (power) factor, 60 cycles	D150	0.05-0.06	0.04-0.06	0.03-0.04
Dissipation (power) factor, 10^3 cycles	D150	0.04-0.06	0.03-0.05	0.02-0.035
Dissipation (power) factor, 10^6 cycles	D150	0.02-0.03	0.02-0.03	0.01-0.02
Arc resistance, sec.	D495	No track	No track	No track
Water absorption, 24 hr., $\frac{1}{8}$-in. thickness, %	D570	0.3-0.4	0.3-0.4	0.2-0.4

Properties of Cast, Molded and Modified Acrylics (*Cont.*)

PROPERTIES	A. S. T. M. TEST METHOD	ACRYLIC — Methyl Methacrylate		Modified Acrylic Molding Compound
		Cast	Molding	
Burning rate	D635	Slow	Slow	Slow
Effect of sunlight	—	Very slight	Very slight	Slight Strength Loss
Effect of weak acids	D543	Practically nil	Practically nil	Practically nil
Effect of strong acids	D543	Attacked only by oxidizing acids and H_2SO_4		Attacked only by oxidizing acids
Effect of weak alkalies	D543	Practically nil	Practically nil	Practically nil
Effect of strong alkalies	D543	Attacked	Attacked	Practically nil
Effect of organic solvents	D543	Soluble in ketones, esters and aromatic chlorinated hydrocarbons. Resistant to alcohols at room temperature		Soluble in ketones, esters, and aromatic hydrocarbons
Machining qualities	—	Fair to excellent	Good to excellent	Good to excellent
Clarity	—	Transparent ($>92\%$ light transmission), translucent, and opaque		Translucent to opaque

* *Modern Plastics Encyclopedia* (Sept. 1959).

EXTRUDING OF ACRYLIC SHEETS AND FORMS

Extrusion of acrylics into sheets, rods and special shapes is comparatively recent, and required development of the art of extrusion to the point where a satisfactory product could be obtained on a competitive basis. Practically all the acrylic extrusion work is a post-war development. Methods for the extrusion of rods and tubes were reported in 1946. The Plax Corporation was a leader in this work. Essentially the same molding powders used for injection molding are used for extrusion. There are, however, some differences, and producers market special grades of molding granules specifically for extrusion.

The important properties of an extruded sheet are uniformity of thickness, lack of built-in stress, freedom from surface defects and an even gloss.

As with injection-molding practice, it is necessary to pre-dry the molding powder to get good results, and this should bring the residual moisture to less than 0.1 per cent. It is also possible to eliminate pre-drying by using a vented extruder. Venting is important in making thicker shapes, such as rods, because it prevents the possibility of the formation of internal bubbles.

Careful control of the melt temperature is required. Some degradation of the powders will occur if the temperature is too high and the product will be somewhat discolored. It is also wise to work at such a temperature that a few minutes' holdup will not cause any discoloration. Manufacturers indicate the best temperature range for their general-purpose and heat-resistant grades of molding powder.

Acrylic powder and its decomposition products are not corrosive and the machine parts can be made of ordinary tool steel. For longer wear characteristics and better finish it is desirable that the critical portions of the machine and die be chrome-plated; this will eliminate such problems as die lines and surface imperfections. A very high polish on the die before plating is desirable.

The thicker the shape extruded, the more important is the problem of bubbling. In the extrusion of rod this problem becomes quite evident unless precautions are taken. The heat-resistant grades will give better results in this respect because they have a lower volatile content and are operated at higher temperatures. To further assist in the elimination of this problem it is well to use a vented extruder barrel with vacuum assist.

Contamination with dust particles will cause dimpling or small sink marks. The marks on the surface are an exaggeration of the dust particle and are very obvious to the eye. Extreme care in housekeeping and filtering of air into the extruder room are helpful. Regrinding must also be done with care to eliminate dust. Running with only virgin material is advisable if the reground powder can be used for less critical products.

The take-off technique is of importance in making a good acrylic extrusion. Air-quenching is used and the cooling should be done slowly. Rapid cooling will cause freeze-off lines across the extrusion and will magnify the size of the dimples. A temperature of the first set of take-off rolls should be between 100 and 130°F. The rolls must also be free of dirt and surface imperfections, as this will cause scratches resembling die lines. To produce a sheet that will exhibit smallest possible shrinkage when postformed it is necessary to draw down the extruded sheet as little as possible at the take-off. This can be accomplished by allowing a small amount of vertical sag between the die and the take-off rolls. This will also help prevent solvent stress cracking and increase impact resistance.

Many manufacturers extrude acrylics on a custom basis for

fairly long runs and a number of them stock the simpler forms of sheets, rods and tubes. The lighting-fixture industry uses large quantities of acrylic extruded shapes, some of which are kept in stock by various companies. The Plax Corp. makes an extruded film of methyl methacrylate known as "Methaflex." This sheet is biaxially oriented or stretched in predetermined ratios in both the transverse and longitudinal direction. This stretching yields a film which is tough in thin sections, has comparatively high rigidity, and excellent dimensional stability and clarity. The sheet is supplied in roll form and can be printed, metallized, coated, stamped and laminated.

The Cadillac Plastics and Chemical Co. extrudes rods, tubes, sheets and shapes in acrylic. This sheet is stocked in colorless and white translucent in thicknesses from .060 to .125 inch. Colors are available on order.

The Southern Plastics Co. stocks sheet up to 62 inches wide and from .040 to .125 inch thick in colorless and translucent grades. They also stock rods up to 2 inches thick and tubes from ⅛ to 5½ inches in diameter. All are available in certain standard colors. The Rotuba Extruders specialize in extruded shapes that are patterned into tiny prism design for the use in lighting fixtures. Over a hundred shapes are available in sizes up to 24 inches wide and the length is limited only by shipping considerations.

DESIGNING AND DECORATING MOLDED AND EXTRUDED ACRYLICS

Many of the products in the field of molded, extruded and cast acrylics are based on interesting optical properties of the product. Use is made of the refraction of light when it enters the plastic and by reflection of light from painted surfaces. By use of these factors in designing the product the light entering one end can be piped through curved and angular portions of the plastic and emerge at the other end with comparatively small loss in intensity. Use of this is made in medical throat lamps, pointers on instruments, and molded parts where edges are made to glow. The use of design to get the maximum of light scattering is of value for the over-all lighting of sign letters, radio dials, and auto taillights.

The most interesting effects are obtained by leaving the front surface of the product untouched and using the back or second surface for all recesses or raised portions. This second surface can then have one color of paint wiped into the hollow and then the entire surface covered with another color. When viewed from the front, the product appears brilliant and the imperfections of the back surface are unnoticed.

The use of color in molded products has infinite possibilities. The molded product can be made in an opaque color or in transparent tints. Color can be applied to the finished molding by spraying, silk screening, rolling and dipping. Use of stencils can be made and colored designs applied. Vacuum metallizing is frequently used on the second surface to produce interesting lustrous gold and gun-metal effects.

Just as cutglass has always been the aristocrat of decorative glass items, so are molded acrylics the aristocrat of the plastics industry. Both have a brilliance and a sparkle inherent in the product itself and the added interest that can be imparted by a designer who understands the material he is working with. In addition to this, the plastic has infinitely more possibilities of color and formability than are possible with glass.

6. ACRYLIC EMULSIONS: MANUFACTURE

The use of plastic resins in liquid form developed rapidly, once the value of solid acrylic plastics had been demonstrated. The first of the liquid acrylic resins to appear on the market were acrylic ester homopolymers made in organic solvents. When these resins were applied to the surface of a textile or other material, the solvent evaporated and left behind the plastic either on the surface or impregnated on the fibers. Many uses for the hard, medium or soft acrylic films were found in the treating and improving of existing products.

These solution polymers had a number of defects that were inherent in the system, and the art of emulsion polymerization evolved as a result of attempts to fit the liquid polymers for more widespread uses and for greater convenience in handling. The solution polymers were of a comparatively low order of molecular weight, and making higher molecular weight polymers involved a lower order of solubility. This, in turn, meant that either the solids content of the resins was lower or the liquid became very viscous and difficult to handle. In the application of these solutions, there was always present the health and fire hazard inherent in the use of organic solvents. Moreover, the solvents had to be evaporated to yield the finished product, and this represented either a total loss of expensive material or the cost of installing and maintaining a solvent recovery system.

Much solution polymer is still sold for specific uses where

101

it serves best and can absorb the extra cost involved. However, the introduction of emulsion polymers served to bring forth many new applications where acrylics in liquid form served well. Discovery of new uses for emulsion polymers continues apace at the present time, and many companies and their technical staffs are devoting much time and money to this end.

EMULSION POLYMERIZATION

An emulsion polymer is defined as a reasonably permanent suspension by use of a surface-active agent of minute particles of polymer in a water medium. If we were able to take a dry polymer and mechanically break it into an impalpable powder and then mix this powder with water containing a suspending agent, we would have made an emulsion polymer. In a few isolated cases this has been done in the polymer field. The reconstitution of powdered milk is a familiar household example. In making acrylic emulsion polymers this method is not feasible. The monomer itself is added directly to the water with other necessary ingredients and polymerization takes place in the monomer phase in the water medium.

The major ingredients that go into the making of an emulsion polymer are the monomers, water, catalyst, and surface-active agent or agents. To this may be added the buffer for pH control, a chain regulator, and perhaps, a dispersing agent and a thickening agent. The mechanism by which it is generally felt that emulsion polymerization takes place is in accordance with the "micelle" theory advanced in 1945 by J. Harkins and further expanded in subsequent years. According to this theory, monomer diffuses from monomer droplets through the water phase into micelles formed by the emulsifier and polymerization takes place within these micelles, forming polymer particles that are surrounded by emulsifier. The site of initiation is in the water phase, and is activated by a water-soluble catalyst. It is also thought that, in the case of less water-soluble monomers, the bulk of the polymerization takes place in the monomer-polymer particles.

Water of zero hardness is now produced for industry quickly and inexpensively by use of ion-exchange resins. Methacrylic acid cross-linked during polymerization is used in this steel mill water purifier. (*Courtesy of The Rohm & Haas Reporter,* **14,** *#2, March-April 1956.*)

The area of emulsion polymerization was known and used before World War II, but was given tremendous impetus by the search for an adequate synthetic rubber to replace loss of natural rubber sources. The United States Government program known as GR-S (government rubber-styrene type) was started in May, 1941, to produce synthetic rubber for war purposes by means of emulsion polymerization. At this time the total synthetic product was about 8000 tons. In 1945, as a result of the need and the tremendous efforts that went into the project, the total reached 700,000 tons. The aftermath of the war led to the spreading of this information and its use by acrylic chemists in their search for better methods of polymerization. To this information was also added the German know-how that was part of the spoils of war and as a result, the art of emulsion polymerization was enormously stimulated in all portions of the vinyl polymer field.

MONOMERS

The monomers used in emulsion polymers may include a very wide variety of mono- or di-functional vinyl materials. Because the medium is an emulsion, both water-soluble and -insoluble monomers may be used almost indiscriminately and the potential number of combinations that have been and are still to be tried is endless. Because of the cost factor, the acrylic monomers most used are ethyl acrylate, methyl methacrylate, and acrylonitrile. Acrylic and methacrylic acid are also used frequently. It is also usual to find vinyl acetate used in combination with the aforementioned acrylic monomers.

In addition to these monomers, many others, some of which are acrylates, are used in smaller quantities to modify in specific ways the polymers normally obtained. Monomers are available with an inhibitor to prevent spontaneous polymerization during transit and handling. For most emulsion polymerizations the monomers may be obtained with a small amount of a special inhibitor, mono-methyl ether of hydroquinone, which is present in the smallest amounts required by safety factors. This monomer can generally be used without removal of the inhibitor by adding a little extra catalyst, possibly with higher temperatures of reaction, to overcome the inhibiting effect. Should removal be necessary, the use of monomer containing hydroquinone is advisable and removal can be accomplished by either distillation or a caustic wash.

CATALYSTS

The use of water-soluble catalysts is indicated in emulsion polymerization. This is in contrast to the use of oil-soluble catalysts in bulk, suspension, and solution polymers. The catalysts most used are the water-soluble peroxides. Hydrogen peroxide, potassium persulfate and ammonium persulfate are the most common. All these catalysts decompose under polymerization conditions and it is frequently necessary to add catalyst from time to time as the polymerization progresses. It is interesting to note that higher concentrations of catalyst usually give higher molecular weights in emulsion polymerization. This is in contrast to bulk and solution polymerization where the opposite holds true, and low concentrations of catalyst are generally desirable.

SURFACE-ACTIVE AGENTS

The system of surface-active agents used in emulsion polymerization is one of the main keys to a successful procedure. During the progress of the polymerization it is called upon to serve a number of different functions, and, although its concentration is quite small, it must be able to perform each of these functions efficiently. At first, it must be a low-foaming and efficient emulsifying agent to break up the monomer into many tiny globules and to keep these globules in dispersion. In this phase it is helped by the agitation in the polymerization unit. When the globules become partly polymerized, they reach a very tacky stage and the surface-active system must function as a protective colloid to prevent the droplets from coagulating.

When polymerization is complete and the product is stored, the surfactant must act as a suspension agent to prevent the solid polymer particles from settling out at the bottom of the storage container. Lastly, when the product is finally used to coat or impregnate another material, it is generally mixed and compounded with a large variety of other chemicals. The surfactant is then called upon to resist the action of these additives both from the chemical point of view and resistance to mechanical shear in the compounding and applying.

All surface-active agents can be divided into three groups depending on their electric charge: they may be (1) anionic, (2) cationic and, (3) if they are not ionizable materials and do not have any electric charge, they are non-ionic. The anionic materials are generally good emulsifiers for use in emulsion polymerization. These are generally sodium or ammonium sulfates or sulfonates of fairly long-chain hydrocarbons. Soaps which are salts of fatty acids were the first surfactants used. This was followed by sulfated and sulfonated soaps such as sodium lauryl sulfate. More recently, we have learned that better materials can be made and more control gained by the addition of up to about 30 moles of ethylene oxide to the hydrocarbon portion of the surfactant molecule. We have also learned that it is not necessary to start with a fatty acid chain, but with completely synthetic materials such as octyl and nonyl phenol. Many of the anionic agents will produce emulsions, but some yield superior emulsion properties. "Aerosol OT," "Triton" X-200 and "Duponol ME" have proved to be good anionic surface-active agents for acrylate polymerization. Cationic agents are used only in isolated cases. For this purpose one of the quaternary ammonium salts is indicated.

The use of non-ionic surfactants is a fairly recent development in emulsion polymer chemistry, and they display advantages over the anionic emulsions in a number of ways. Their electrical stability allows the user of the resin to add salts in the compounding with much less danger of breaking the emulsion. Other chemicals or emulsions that may be anionic or cationic can be also added, and the use of hard water in dilution is possible without the salting out and agglomeration that would take place with anionic emulsions. Non-ionic surfactants are of a number of chemical types. The most useful for emulsion work are alcohols of long chain alkyl or alkyl-aryl hydrocarbons reacted with varying amounts of ethylene oxide. Various of the "Triton" OPE series, "Tergitols," "Igepals," and others have proved useful. Non-ionic polymerizations run under redox generally yield better emulsions than if run at reflux conditions.

An emulsifier consists of two distinct chemical parts—a hydrophilic head and a hydrophobic tail. It does its work in an oil-in-water emulsion by surrounding the oil droplet and keeping it separated from the other oil drops dispersed in the water phase. The molecules of emulsifier orient themselves around this oil drop with their hydrophilic heads pointing toward the water phase and their hydrophobic tails pointing toward the oil phase. For all emulsion work, a balance of hydrophilic and hydrophobic properties is needed, but this balance changes from system to system. For acrylic emulsion polymerization this balance is best weighted toward the hydrophilic end. Those surfactants that have comparatively long ethylene oxide adducts produce the best results. However, it should be understood that the more hydrophilic the surfactant, the less water-resistant is the dry polymer. For this reason it is also desirable to keep the total amount of surfactant used as low as possible.

There are many anionic emulsions on the market today, but they are generally being replaced by more stable non-ionics. Many of the available emulsions use combinations of partly anionic and partly non-ionic surfactants. These are thoroughly good emulsions, exhibit high degrees of chemical and mechanical stability, and should be judged by the end user as to performance and not as to electrical charge.

Control of the pH conditions during polymerization is often desirable, and the addition of a buffer is indicated. Small amounts of sodium carbonate or bicarbonate can serve. This will neutralize the small amounts of free acid present in the monomers. Under alkaline conditions a fairly rapid hydrolysis of the monomer takes place and it is desirable to run acrylate polymerizations at a pH of 7 or less. Where lower or narrower ranges of molecular weight are desired it is generally accomplished by the addition of a small amount of a chain terminator. For water emulsion a mercaptan such as mercapto-succinic acid is used.

Although a reasonably soft water will produce a good emulsion, it is to the advantage of the manufacturer to use de-ionized water. This will lower the salt content of the product, allow for better reproducibility and smaller particle size. It also gives the user a little more leeway in his compounding.

REFLUX AND REDOX

There are two major variations in the polymerization procedure, namely, reflux or redox. In any given monomer system in water, the monomer will boil within a determinable temperature range. Polymerizations run in this temperature range are being run "at reflux." If the temperature of reaction is just below this reflux range, a sharp difference in the rate of polymerization is usually evident, due to the inhibiting effect of the oxygen in the polymerization unit. This oxygen can greatly lengthen the induction period before the polymerization starts and also slow down the rate of polymerization. The vapor caused by the boiling replaces the air under reflux conditions and polymerization can proceed rapidly and evenly. Should it be desirable to run at a temperature below the reflux point, it is necessary to replace the air by sparging or blanketing with an inert gas such as nitrogen or carbon dioxide.

Because it was found that higher temperatures of polymerization lead to lower molecular weight polymers, attempts were made sucessfully to use a catalyst-activator system that would operate well in the lower temperature ranges. The knowledge gained from the GR-S synthetic rubber program was used for this work and redox methods were developed. "Redox" is a contraction of "reduction-oxidation." The oxidant used is the usual persulfate catalyst, and the reducing agent that serves as the activator is usually a sulfoxy compound or a small amount of ferrous salt. Sulfoxy compounds frequently used are sodium metabisulfite, thiosulfite and hydrosulfite. Polymerizations are easily carried out with redox systems at room temperature or below, there is no need for a condenser, and the induction period is small. Under these conditions it is desirable to flush with an inert gas, as mentioned above.

Acrylic polymerizations are all highly exothermic. For this reason it is almost impossible, especially in large reactors, to add all the monomer to the water at the beginning and let it go. Where it would generally go is straight up the vent—and violently. What happens is that the volume of water in the process and the cooling capacity of the jacket are insufficient to remove the heat of reaction; the temperature rises rapidly and this in turn speeds up the polymerization, giving off larger amounts of heat. The kettle contents rapidly goes beyond the boiling point and the batch is lost.

To prevent this, all or large portions of the monomers are added to the batch by a method of slow addition. This allows the heat generated to be removed by cooling and the amount of heat that has to be removed is controlled by the rate of addition of fresh monomer to the batch. This addition

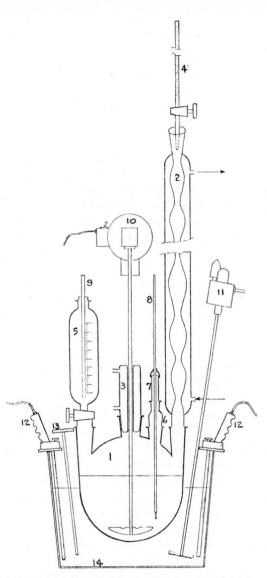

Laboratory apparatus for emulsion polymerization. (See identification code on opposite page.)

technique may be varied by emulsifying the monomer and adding the emulsion to the kettle, and it is sometimes advantageous to disperse part of the emulsifier or one part of the emulsifier system in the addition monomers.

AGITATION

Agitation is an important factor in producing good emulsions. A great deal has been said on this subject and many directly opposite suggestions have been made. One method advocates the use of a turbo-type agitator; another uses a slow paddle system. Some reasonable generalizations can be made. First, any agitation that causes foaming is bad. This foam will dry and precipitate out as floc. High shear will cause a breaking of the emulsion at the critical tacky stage because it will buck the dispersing and protective action of the surfactant. Too low an agitator speed or too inefficient an agitator will not rapidly emulsify the monomer being added, and will allow pooling of the monomer and result in very poor and grainy emulsions. In broad terms the best agitation would be one in which there is high turbulence and low shear. It should also be noted that the shape of the vessel and size of batch also affect the product. The best way to work out the problem is in a given vessel and with a given batch size and agitator.

When the polymerization is completed, some small amount of residual monomer remains. This monomer, even though it may be less than 1 per cent of the total, leaves an undesirable smell and should be removed. This can be done by the addition of a little redox catalyst or by steam distillation. If the amount is quite small, it is possible to remove the odor by blowing an inert gas through the vessel. Rarely, in acrylate polymerization, is it economically feasible to recover this unpolymerized material. This is in contrast to synthetic rubber polymerization, where the rate of conversion becomes so slow at any early stage, that the usual procedure is to carry the polymerization just so far, and then recover the remaining monomer, which is subsequently used again.

EXAMPLE OF AN EMULSION POLYMERIZATION

A typical example of a laboratory batch of an acrylic emulsion polymerization follows:

Scope: This procedure describes the preparation of an ethyl acrylate-methyl methacrylate-methacrylic acid terpolymer system. A delayed addition of monomer and redox catalyst system is used. The surfactant system is a one element anionic material.

Chemicals

	% by Weight
Ethyl acrylate (200 ppm MEHQ)	29.26
Methyl methacrylate (100 ppm MEHQ)	14.41
Methacrylic acid (1000 ppm HQ)	0.67
"Triton" X-200 (28%)	11.57
Sodium bicarbonate	0.05
Ammonium persulfate solution (4%)	2.42
Sodium metabisulfite solution (10%)	1.00
Water (deionized)	40.34
"Acrysol" ASE-75 (40%)	0.28
	100.00
Per cent solids calculated	47.94

Suggested Uses: Latex vehicle for water based paints, leather coatings, pigment binder in textile printing, clay binder in paper coatings and upholstery backing finishes.

Procedure

1. Add to the vessel the surfactant, "Triton" X-200; the buffer, sodium bicarbonate; water and 35 per cent of a mixture of the three monomers.
2. Sparge system with prepurified nitrogen.
3. After 15 minutes of sparging, add, in order, the persulfate and metabisulfite catalyst solutions.
4. The temperature will start to rise on its own exothermic heat of reaction, at which time the delayed monomer addition is started. (Nitrogen may be stopped at this point.)
5. Maintain a reaction temperature between 30 and 60°C throughout the addition period of 1½ to 2 hours.
6. After the delayed monomer addition is completed, allow reaction exotherm to dissipate. Then heat slowly to 90°C, hold for one hour to complete the polymerization and cool to room temperature.
7. Add Acrysol ASE-75 and raise the pH to 8.5 to 9.0 with 28 per cent ammonium hydroxide.

Average Physical Properties

Brookfield Viscosity at $73 \pm 1°C$, 3 spindle, 20 rpm	400 centipoises
% solids (actual)	47.0
pH	8.6

If a low viscosity emulsion is desired, the addition of the "Acrysol" ASE-75 should be omitted.

This same reaction could have been run at reflux conditions. The sodium metabisulfite would be omitted and the temperature would be maintained at about 80°C throughout the run.

7. MANUFACTURE OF SOLUTION POLYMERS

The first of the acrylic resins to be exploited for commercial purposes were the solution polymers. These were homopolymers of the acrylic esters in various organic solvents. The softer and tackier polymers were suggested as useful for adhesives and the tougher polymers for use as coatings for various purposes. Blending any two of these polymers would yield a series of resins with intermediate properties. Although thirty years or so have passed since these first products were made available, and much has been learned about the possibilities of manufacture and usage, many of the solution polymers sold today are very much the same as the first products made.

CHOICE OF MONOMERS

Many factors enter into the preparation of a solution polymer for a particular end use. First there is the problem of what system of monomers to polymerize to serve the purpose best. Because of the cost considerations, it is natural that the choice should be with the lower acrylic and methacrylic esters. Many of the available solution polymers do contain just the lower esters. But the use of less expensive vinyl compounds and styrene can still further lower the cost of the product. Of course, this may affect the color and lower the

114

weather resistance of the product, but where the cost is the deciding factor, many solution polymers do contain varying quantities of these less expensive monomers. Smaller quantities of various more expensive monomers are used where the end use demands it in order to up-grade the product and add such specific properties as extreme toughness, very high tack or the ability to cross-link after application. It should be understood that in solution polymers, cross-linking must take place after treating because otherwise the resin would not remain in solution.

SOLVENT SYSTEMS

The problem of what solvent or solvent system to use is another factor. First, it must be understood that solvents act as chain terminators and the molecular weight of the product is a function of what solvent is used and in what concentration. The choice of solvent also depends on its cost. The user of a solution polymer either drives off the solvent into the air, in which case it is a total loss, or invests in expensive solvent recovery systems. It would be quite simple if the lowest cost solvent would serve in every case; but more expensive solvents are often necessary because they will be better solvents for the polymer and will permit making and handling of resins which are higher in solids content. Some solvents will be more useful because the percent of monomer converted to polymer in a reasonable manufacturing time will be greater. In other cases the solvent will allow higher molecular weight polymers and therefore, possibly better resin properties. The important question of the flash point of the solvent and its fire hazard are also determining factors.

The molecular weight of the polymer is an important factor in solution polymers. Because of the nature of the operation and the chain-terminating properties of the solvent, solution polymers are generally restricted in the range of medium to low molecular weights. If higher molecular weights were obtained, the solution would be quite viscous and difficult to handle. If the solvent is not good enough as a solvent for the particular system, gelation will occur and spoil the product. But the superior properties of the higher molecular weight products and the desire to get as high a solids content as possible generally lead to use of many solution polymers that are quite viscous and frequently have to be cut back for use.

The solvent most widely used in solution polymers is toluene. It is low in cost, with a moderate flash point, and quite inexpensive. It is also a fairly good solvent for most of the acrylic esters. Benzene and butyl acetate are better solvents and will yield higher molecular weight polymers, but the toxicity of benzene generally rules it out and butyl acetate is high in cost. Acetone is often used because of its reasonable cost and good solubility characteristics, but it is a fire hazard and can only be used with extreme care. Other solvents used are ethyl acetate, methyl isobutyl ketone, cellosolve acetate and others. Various proprietary coal tar and petroleum hydrocarbons such as naphtha are also useful solvents for polymerization.

The ratio of solvent to monomer in the process is related to the molecular weight of the polymer obtained. The more monomer and the less solvent the higher the molecular weight. This will, however, build up the viscosity of the solution during the process to a high degree and will slow down the conversion. It is common practice to start with a high monomer concentration and then at some point dilute with more solvent to get a product with a fair molecular weight and good conversion to polymer.

TEMPERATURE CONDITIONS

The effect of the temperature of polymerization on the resulting polymer is marked. The molecular weight of the polymer is indirectly proportional to the reaction temperature. Higher temperatures will result in lower polymer weights, and it is advantageous to run at lower temperatures.

This brings in the problem of the reflux point of the solvent employed and the inhibiting effect of oxygen. For convenience it would be easiest to operate at reflux temperature. This would permit simple control and reproducibility of operation, and the head of solvent vapor would exclude the oxygen from the operation. If a low-boiling solvent such as acetone or ethyl acetate is used, the low temperature allows a yield of a fairly high weight polymer. Should the solvent be a high boiler such as toluene or butyl acetate, then a low molecular weight polymer would result. For this case, it is necessary to operate at a lower temperature than reflux and use an atmosphere of inert gas to exclude oxygen.

As with other polymerization methods, the exotherm during the procedure is a factor. Under reflux, vapor phase cooling in the condenser is a great help in the removal of exothermic heat. At temperatures below reflux, all the heat must be removed by the cooling capacity of the jacket. For monomer systems that polymerize rapidly, heat removal becomes a problem, particularly for low-boiling solvents. It is sometimes necessary to add the monomer over a period of time to control the amount of exotherm and match it to the cooling capacity of the equipment. As a consequence of this method of operation, the product is of low molecular weight because a high ratio of solvent to monomer is always present in the system. With monomer systems that normally polymerize slowly and therefore give off heat at a lower rate, the monomer can be added at the beginning of the operation, heat can be removed by adequate cooling, and the process will yield polymer of higher molecular weight.

CATALYSTS

Although the persulfates are efficient catalysts, they cannot be used in organic solvent polymerization because they are insoluble under these conditions. Benzoyl peroxide is the most frequently used catalyst, although azobisisobutyronitrile, *t*-butyl hydroperoxide and other solvent-soluble peroxides are also used. The more catalyst used, the lower will be the molecular weight of the polymer. It therefore stands to reason that lower catalyst content is desirable. However, the catalyst is used up in the operation by the length of time of polymerization and the temperature of the operation. At higher temperatures of operation, higher catalyst concentrations are needed. When slow addition of the monomer is used as a method of operating, the catalyst can be added to the monomer and fresh catalyst would then be added in proportion to the monomer. When the monomer is added at the start of the operation, small additions of catalyst can be made throughout the polymerization period, as needed. The particular catalyst used enters the picture because different catalysts decompose at different rates. Benzoyl peroxide, although an efficient catalyst, decomposes quite rapidly, particularly at higher temperatures. *t*-Butyl hydroperoxide will decompose more slowly and is not as much affected by higher temperatures.

In emulsion polymerization of acrylates, the problem of converting all the monomer to polymer is not very difficult. Conversion of more than 99 per cent of the monomer can be easily achieved in a reasonable time. The small amount of residual monomer can be removed or forced to polymerize by higher heat or redox catalyst. This does not hold true for many systems of solution polymers. Conversion from monomer to polymer at the start of the polymerization proceeds at a rapid rate; but depending on the solvent, viscosity, and monomers involved, this rate of conversion may show up

Experimental reactor for solution polymerization of vinyl-type monomers. A slow speed, anchor-type agitator and controlled jacket temperature are important features. Vapor phase cooling in a large condenser is used to control exotherm. (*Courtesy of Catalin Corp. of America.*)

greatly. The result is that solution polymerization cycles are frequently quite lengthy. Choice of solvent, catalyst, and method of operation can help with the time factor, but the final product may contain an appreciable amount of unpolymerized monomers. These monomers will evaporate with the solvent during application.

Manufacturing equipment for solution polymerization is carried out in stainless steel or glass-lined equipment. The agitator for viscous materials is of the anchor type with a bottom bearing, and the clearance between the agitator and the side wall is kept as small as possible to prevent a build-up of resin on the wall and consequent poor heat transfer. The jacket and condenser are designed to give maximum cooling, and the condenser must be adequate to prevent any excessive loss of solvent during the long operation cycle.

Control is carried out by regular sampling of the batch and its progress is observed by checking the viscosity and the solids. The percent solids indicates the conversion and the viscosity is an indication of the molecular weight of the polymer. Addition of more solvent at the propitious time can control the molecular weight within limits, and changing the cycle length to attain the desired conversion can control the solids content.

EXAMPLE OF A SOLUTION POLYMERIZATION

Monomers supplied at high inhibitor levels are washed with caustic to remove this inhibitor. Monomers supplied with low levels of inhibitor, particularly those with the methyl ether of hydroquinone as the inhibitor can generally be used for polymerization as is. A somewhat longer induction period and need for more catalyst to overcome the effect of the inhibitor may be necessary.

The following laboratory example of a solution polymerization of an ethyl acrylate homopolymer in toluene will further demonstrate some of the techniques and problems mentioned previously. The product is a comparatively low viscosity polymer with low molecular weight. Conversion of monomer to polymer goes to virtual completion in the indicated time of reaction. The product is useful where a soft, extensible and slightly tacky coating material would be needed. It is suggested for use in adhesives, as a base coating for metal surfaces and textiles and as a plasticizing resin for nitrocellulose lacquers.

Formulation:

Ethyl acrylate HQ inhibited	39.8%
Nitration grade toluene	59.7%
Benzoyl peroxide	0.5%

Procedure:

1. Wash the hydroquinone inhibitor from the ethyl acrylate according to standard procedure.
2. Dissolve ⅗ of the catalyst in the washed monomer.
3. Charge the toluene and ⅕ of the catalyst to the reaction flask. Raise temperature to 95°C. Maintain a nitrogen blanket over the materials during the polymerization.
4. Add the catalyzed monomer to the heated toluene at a rate of approximately 1 cc per minute, maintaining the temperature of 95°C throughout. Note that the catalyzed monomer should be used immediately and kept from getting warm during the addition to prevent polymerization before addition to the flask.
5. React at 95°C for 4 hours.
6. Add the remaining ⅕ catalyst and polymerize for 4 hours more. This will polymerize the small amount of monomer left after the completion of the addition.

The total reaction time is 8 hours. This product will yield a 40 per cent solids resin with a viscosity of 55 centipoises at 30°C.

The same procedure run at a temperature of 100°C would yield the same conversion in about half the time and the viscosity would be about half that of the example. Less catalyst would give somewhat lower conversions in the same time but the resin would have a higher molecular weight and higher viscosity. A similar reaction, but run with a 50 per cent concentration of monomer rather than 40 per cent and finally cut back to 40 per cent would yield a much higher molecular weight polymer and a viscosity in the neighborhood of 10,000 to 20,000 centipoises. For this case, it would be necessary to extend the total time of reaction to get a good conversion and extra catalyst additions would be needed throughout the polymerization period.

8. APPLICATIONS OF EMULSIONS AND SOLUTIONS

A list of the acrylic emulsions and solutions available to the manufacturer would easily reach into the hundreds, especially if all the specialty resins were included. For the purpose of classifying and understanding the properties of these resins numerous tests are used, both on the resin and on the films produced from them. An understanding of these testing procedures and their comparative results will enable the user to determine which of the products available may best suit his purpose. After the field of possible resins has been narrowed to the few whose properties seem to fit the needs, an evaluation must be made in actual production tests. This will generally eliminate all but a few resins and the final decision will probably be determined by price.

EVALUATING THE EMULSION

The evaluation of acrylic emulsions in their emulsion form before drying involves up to about twenty tests. The appearance of the emulsion to the experienced eye will tell a good deal. The average particle size of the emulsion particle ranges from 0.01 micron to about 5 microns. A chalky appearing white emulsion generally is of a particle size above 1 micron. In the ½ to 1 micron range the emulsion will take on a bluish opalescence and, if spread thinly, will be semi-transparent. Below ½ micron this opalescence will increase and the emulsion will tend to become viscous and somewhat thixotropic. It will also tend to flocculate easily and show poor stability, unless the solids content is lowered. In some emulsions the color tends toward a yellow or red, rather than a bluish caste. This coloration may be due to the surfactant or the use of other than acrylic monomers. This color will tend to show up in the dried film and may be undesirable for some uses.

Acrylic emulsions usually have some odor and the experienced nose can determine whether there is more than a minimum of residual monomer in the emulsion. The penetrating and pungent smell of the monomers is quite annoying to those not accustomed to it, and the manufacturer of the emulsion takes pains to remove traces of the monomer. In those cases where this is difficult or costly, it is not unusual to add a more pleasant covering odor. It should be noted that when the emulsion has been applied and dried, the odor usually disappears completely. Less than 1 per cent of free monomer in an emulsion is generally considered acceptable for most uses.

Routine check of the pH of the emulsion and its specific gravity at about 25°C is made. The pH of emulsions will vary all the way from about 3 to 10. All monomers have small amounts of free acid in their composition and unless buffers or neutralizers are added at some point in their manufacture, the emulsion will be acid, and this will cause rusting of equipment. It is best to ship emulsions at a pH close to the neutral point and any changes can easily be made by the user. The specific gravity is usually expressed in pounds per gallon to allow for ease in calculation.

The viscosity of emulsions is usually measured on a Brookfield Viscometer. In order to get comparable results it is necessary to use the same temperature, spindle and rpm in conducting these viscosity tests. A change of the spindle size and the rpm will often give quite different results. This difference is due to the fact that not many emulsions have a thixotropic index of about 1.00 but show more or less indication of non-Newtonian flow. For high-speed machine operations the non-Newtonian flow can cause clogging of the machine and build-up of resin on the moving parts. It is wise to obtain some indication of the thixotropic index of the resin to be used so that an indication of possible processing difficulties can be predetermined.

The measurement of particle size of emulsion particles is done with an electron microscope, which shows the range of size of the emulsion particles. By count and measurement the average size can be determined. It is of interest to note that a narrow range of particle size is not necessarily a criterion of a good emulsion. Some emulsions of wide size range are satisfactory and, oddly enough, may have excellent flow characteristics. This phenomenon is not too well understood. The ordinary microscope is also useful in determining particle size. Sizes of above 1 micron can be seen with the optical microscope and the size measured. Below this range, an empirical idea of particle size can be obtained by observation of the Brownian movement. Average particle size can also be determined empirically by the use of a light-scattering apparatus and measurement of light intensity from a constant source that is passed through a cell containing a standard thickness and concentration of the emulsion. Correlation of the light-scattering data with a number of known standards makes for a rapid method of determining average particle size.

Measurement of the molecular weight of the polymer is a good indicator of its properties and shows the average size of the length of the chain and its branches and cross links. The molding properties, nature of the film strength and toughness are all indicated by the molecular weight. It is also an excellent check of how consistent a resin is from batch to batch. Many ways of determining molecular weight have been used. Among these are measurement of light scattering, sedimentation by ultracentrifuge, precipitation with non-solvents and measurement of osmotic pressure. For routing checks, the simplest method is by determination of viscosity of very dilute solution in a given solvent. The determination of the viscosity of a few samples at different concentrations is made using a modified Ostwald-type viscosimeter. The Ostwald viscosity divided by the concentration is then plotted as a ratio and the curve extrapolated to zero. Where this curve cuts the axis at zero concentration is called the specific viscosity. This is directly related to the molecular weight of the polymer, and a comparison of intrinsic viscosities of various resins is a good indication of their nature.

An emulsion is by its nature a heterogeneous system. The water phase, which is continuous, has a non-continuous polymer phase dispersed in it. The stability of the system as is, and when various disruptive forces act on it, is a matter that must be carefully considered. The first disruptive force is that of gravity, which tends to settle the heavier polymer particles to the bottom of the liquid. A good emulsion should show negligible settling on extended storage at normal temperatures. Shelf life of more than a year with negligible settling is quite common with acrylic emulsions. Accelerated testing for settling is done by diluting the emulsion with water to a low solids content, and observing the settling in a burette. The sedimentation can easily be observed over a period of a few days and the result read directly from the burette in milliliters. The continuous molecular movement in the emulsion can cause coagulation of the polymer in a poorly dispersed system. Measurement of the amount of flocculation from time to time can indicate this factor.

In the normal course of the shipping and storing of emulsions they may be subjected to temperatures below the freezing point of water. Emulsions can stand temperatures up to a few degrees below the freezing point because of the freezing point depression caused by the salts they contain in the water phase. However, if an unprotected emulsion should freeze, it represents a complete loss because it will not return to emulsion form on thawing, but remains as an agglomerated mass of wet polymer. This characteristic can cause sudden and serious losses of resin. Much work has been done to prevent freezing from breaking the emulsion. Some surfactant systems have been found to improve this failing and use is made of various antifreeze compounds to prevent "hard-freeze." The testing of freeze-thaw properties is done by subjecting the emulsion to a cycle of freezing followed by thawing at room temperature. The process is repeated through a number of cycles until flocculation occurs. The temperature of the freeze cycle may range from -5 to $-20°C$ and is reported in number of cycles of freezing and thawing before failure. A resin that passes five such cycles at $-15°C$ is considered good. It should be understood that even freeze-resistant emulsion should be kept from freezing because each freezing will cause a coarsening of the polymer particles and an increase of the average particle size.

Shearing forces of a mechanical nature are commonly applied to emulsions during the course of mixing into compound treating baths and in mechanical application of the bath during impregnation or coating. If these shearing forces are greater than the dispersing power of the emulsion, coagulation takes place and the polymer will build up on the equipment and processing will be uneven. Testing of the mechanical stability of emulsions can be done quickly by subjecting them to the action of a high-speed mixer, such as a Waring Blender, for a 10 or 15 minute period and then filtering to measure the amount of flocculation. Another method of comparative testing is to subject the resins to a week in a ball mill and compare the amount thrown out of emulsion.

In making up treating baths in which acrylic emulsions play a part, the emulsion is subjected to chemical stresses which may cause it to break. Before the use of the non-ionic emulsifiers, the emulsions were quite limited in respect to compounding ingredients. Any substance that would neutralize the charge on the emulsifier would cause complete flocculation of the polymer. The use of the non-ionics, care in particle size control, and better balanced systems have made the modern emulsions highly resistant to chemical shock and have greatly extended the type and amount of additives that can be used. They can even stand blending with polyvalent metal ions, which are about the worst offender.

Testing of chemical stability is best done by making up a sample treating bath and observing its stability. Routine testing by the emulsion supplier usually includes tests in which a dilute emulsion and a dilute salt are mixed in equal proportions. If there is no flocculation, the test is satisfactory. Alum, sodium chloride and borax are examples of salts that might be used for this test. Another test is the ability of an emulsion to take up varying quantities of organic solvents and keep its stability. If there is sufficient emulsifier in the product, this test is generally satisfactory. It may also be of interest to check out the pH range over which the emulsion is stable. This should be done by the slow and careful addition of diluted acids or alkalies.

EVALUATING THE POLYMER FILM

After an emulsion has proved satisfactory for the application it is to be used for, the properties of the polymer film should be examined. There are a number of ways of making a film. If the emulsion or treating bath is thick enough to spread evenly in thin sections and not flow, then the film may easily be made by some standard film-spreading devices which can be adjusted to the desired film thickness. A piece of plate glass is an excellent base for film casting, but many emulsions adhere to glass and are difficult to remove for testing without damage. A melamine-treated paper held flat on a vacuum plate will give a good film and the polymer will not adhere to the melamine surface. Low-viscosity emulsions that would flow out on a flat surface can be cast on glass by drawing an outline of a certain size with a china marking pencil and then pouring into this outline a weighed amount of the emulsion. The wax will stop the flow of the liquid and a film of desired thickness will result. Another method suggests the casting of films on the surface of a dish of mercury.

Much valuable empirical information can be gained by observation of the drying of the emulsion into a film. Total drying time at room temperature and under elevated temperatures will give indication of how it would act in production. Observation of the degree of transparency of the emulsion in thin sections will indicate particle size, as mentioned previously, and any agglomerates and impurities will show up easily.

The total drying time of a given thickness of film is taken when the milkiness disappears from the film. In a thin section, say 1 or 2 mils, this takes only about 10 minutes. Some emulsions, particularly in thicker sections, tend to form a film on the surface that is quite impervious and impedes further drying of the moisture entrapped. This may present a treating problem, but these emulsions will have better resistance to moisture when they are dried. The dry film is examined for its brilliance, clarity and lack of haze.

In the course of the drying of a film-forming emulsion, the

Acrylic Resins

polymer particles should fuse together into a continuous film. Under a lens, relative degrees of graininess of the film can be observed that would be invisible to the eye. It should be noted that the formation of a film is a function of the temperature. Many emulsions that are relatively nonfilm-forming at room temperature will form excellent films at temperatures normally used in forced drying.

The surface glossiness of a film can be measured by a glossmeter which determines the amount of light reflected from the film surface at a particular angle. The usual angle is 60° and the instrument is known as the "60° specular gloss meter." This quality is particularly important in such applications as floor waxes.

Films that are self-supporting can be cut to a standard size and the tensile strength and elongation properties can be determined with a tensile tester such as the Scott Tester, which was developed for paper testing. The instrument draws a graph of the pounds of pull versus the elongation. Both figures can be read from the graph and interesting data can also be gained from comparing the types of curves given by different films. In some resins the break at the ultimate tensile point is quite sharp. Other resins are more elastic and the slope of the curve and rate of climb change quite slowly. Many of the softer acrylic films are soft and quite tacky, making it difficult, if not impossible, to get a piece of self-supporting film that can be put on the tensile tester. For these emulsions, instead of working with the film, one can impregnate a piece of paper with high absorbency with the emulsion and allow it to dry. The paper is then cut to a convenient size and placed in the tensile tester. With equivalent amount of resin pick-up on the paper, the results from resin to resin are quite significant and serve as an excellent means of comparison.

The surface hardness of a film is measured by the Sward hardness tester. This standard device consists of a flat plate on which the film is cast and a rocker which is placed on the film. The rocker is very accurately balanced and machined and is the heart of the apparatus. The rocker is started oscillating and the oscillations are counted. The harder the surface of the film, the less the oscillations will change in amplitude during a given time. In a softer material the rocker will sink into the film to some extent and will be going "uphill" as it rolls back and forth. This will slow up the amplitude of the oscillations more rapidly. Comparison of these differences in arbitrary numbers constitutes the "Sward Rocker Hardness" of the film. Plate glass hardness is used as a standard.

The abrasion resistance of a film is measured dry with the Taber abrasion tester. Depending on the application, this can measure the ease of scratching of the surface and consequent loss of light transmittance or it can be carried to the failure point of the film and measure how much ultimate resistance to tearing the film has. Wet testing is done by a scrub tester. The film is held on the bottom surface of a pan; water or detergent solutions are placed in the pan to cover the film, and a bristle brush with a reciprocating action is rubbed back and forth over the film. Failure of the surface is observed and measured in brushing cycles.

The "blocking" of films is their property of adhering to themselves. Many otherwise excellent resins cannot be used for various coating operations, such as for paper and fabric, because they will stick together. This is particularly severe under elevated temperature conditions, and many coated products come off the dryers still warm and are stacked or rolled. To test this fault in a resin, the piece of film is doubled over and placed under a standard weight for a length of time at a specific temperature. The weight is then removed and the film cooled. The film is then unfolded and the amount of blocking is judged empirically as severe, moderate, or excellent.

Resistance of the film to water is judged in two ways. The blush, or water spotting resistance, is judged by placing a drop of water on the film and observing the amount of blush or whitening that occurs in a certain time. Quantitative judging of this property can be done by measuring the amount of change in light transmittance with a photocell. The film may not be appreciably weakened by the water application and the blushing may be only a surface phenomenon and of very little consequence in many applications. Actual weakening of the film and swelling due to water absorption are measured by cutting a film into standard sized pieces, and boiling them in water. The films are then removed and weighed after blotting for the amount of water absorbed and measured for change in size or areal swell. The water resistance of films from acrylic emulsions varies over a wide range, but none are really waterproof.

The resistance of thermoplastic films to the action of organic solvents is quite poor, but many of the cross-linked products exhibit good solvent resistance after curing. Measurement of this resistance is judged by the amount of swelling caused by immersion of the film in the solvent at various temperatures. Test solvents are of three classes—a straight aliphatic, a mixture of aliphatic and aromatic, and an aromatic only.

The testing procedures described are general in nature, and a number of more empirical tests are used to determine the applicability of an emulsion for a specific end use. Some of these will be mentioned as part of the discussion of the different types of applications. Each applications chemist must of necessity, from time to time, devise tests that will serve to give information concerning the project at hand. Where possible, use is made of standard test methods as described by the ASTM and the AATCC, etc., but in many instances there are no standard tests.

The bulk of the described tests for emulsions and their films serve equally well for the testing of acrylic solutions and their films. Being true solutions, the problems of thixotropicity and stability are not generally involved. The appearance as to color and transparency is easily observed and any impurities such as foreign matter show up immediately. Films of solutions tend to retain a small amount of solvent after drying, and it is of interest to check this property and determine the optimum time and temperature for complete solvent evaporation. Compatibility of the solution with other resins is usually of interest, and it should be noted that films of acrylics solutions are truly waterproof. Solution polymers that cross-link on curing are checked for re-solubility and degree of cross-link.

APPLICATIONS

Acrylic resins have found wide use as base materials for the treatment of fabric, paper, leather and as protective and decorative coatings. Superior adhesives of many types are based on acrylic resin formulations. Their use in the making of artificial fibers has made enormous strides.

Any comprehensive listing of the many uses for acrylic resins would, of necessity be quite lengthy but indication of the application in some of the major uses will indicate the versatility of the plastic.

Textiles

Until a few years ago, the modification of textiles was done by the application of natural materials such as starches, natural gums and gelatins. Today the textile industry employs a large variety of synthetic polymers that impart properties impossible to obtain with natural products.

The acrylic family constitutes one of the rapidly advancing

groups of these synthetics. The application of acrylic resins can change the feel and body (or "hand") of the fabric over a wide range. Flimsy fabrics can be given a firm, full hand and a heavy body by their use. Weak fibers or weaves can be increased in tensile strength and made to hold their shape with resin treatment. Fraying can be lessened for long periods of use and repeated washings. Permanent stiffening or "starching" of the fabric can be accomplished by acrylic resin treatment.

As contrasted with the natural products and with other synthetic systems, the acrylics can impart these desirable modifications and still not change the appearance of the fabric, because of their transparency. Exposure to light and heat will cause no appreciable change in the resin. They are not subject to bacterial action or mildew and are resistant to grease and oil. The flexibility of the resin is a permanent feature and is not subject to the less permanent effect of a plasticizer. It is also interesting to note that moisture taken up by textiles treated with acrylic emulsions is the same as that of untreated fabric.

Chlorination during washing is a major cause of the weakening of fabrics treated with some synthetics. The chlorine becomes a fixed part of the fiber and slowly evolves hydrochloric acid that weakens the fiber. Acrylics will not fix the chlorine in the fabric. Acrylics for fabric treating are in their final form before treatment, as contrasted with other synthetics that are catalyzed and polymerized after treating the fabric. These catalysts generally have a corrosive action.

Less costly vinyl emulsions used on fabrics will not show the wash-fastness of acrylics and will yellow on aging. Aside from this, they have properties similar to the acrylics, and many emulsions used are vinyl resins plasticized with higher acrylates. Loss of quality is made up for by lower cost.

The popular crease-resistant and wash-wear finishes are

made by treating the fabric with thermosetting resins. The incorporation of a compatible acrylic emulsion will improve the crease resistance and strengthen the tensile properties of the fabric. Up to about 5 per cent of the acrylic is recommended. This can be used also with hand builders such as polyvinyl alcohol.

The continuous flexing and abrasion of fabrics during use lead to eventual failure. The use of acrylic resin treatment greatly extends the useful life of the fabric. This added abrasion and flex resistance is true in both wet and dry states.

The very hard acrylic emulsions, containing high proportions of methyl methacrylate, will not form films on drying. The resins are useful as delustering agents for fabrics. The minute particles of polymer will impregnate the fiber and dry to form an efficient light-scattering surface.

A few illustrations on specific fabrics will illustrate the use of acrylic treatments. A fairly hard and firm acrylic emulsion treatment will give broadcloth a smooth hand. Sheeting and percales can be given a full finish by the use of a medium-hard and flexible resin. A soft and elastic resin can impart a full hand to worsted and improve its shape-retaining qualities. On acetates the use of acrylics of the softer types will improve the mark-off and impart a full hand.

In many cases the acrylic emulsion may be used as received or just diluted with water. It may also be compounded with additional wetting agent for better penetration, and with such common textile finishing materials as starch, borax, etc. Where less penetration and a heavier surface treatment are desired, the emulsion may be thickened with salts of polyacrylic acid, a variety of methyl cellulose products and alginates. Many acrylic emulsions have already incorporated into the polymer chain a small per cent of polyacrylic acid. By simply adding small amounts of alkali such as ammonia, these emulsions can be thickened from a few centipoises to about 30 poises. By controlling the solids content of the mix and the pH, intermediate viscosities can be obtained.

Impregnation of the fabric can be done by the use of the padder or mangle. Drying fixes the resin on the fabric. In many instances, the dyeing and finishing may be done in one pass by formulating a suitable bath. A suitable coater can be used for the treatment of one or both sides of the fabric in those cases where a surface treatment is wanted.

The back-coating of upholstery fabrics by acrylic emulsions has been widely accepted. They impart a full, soft hand to the fabric and greatly increase its life. They also help to improve the depth of color of dyed fabrics. Where the fabric is dyed after back-coating, strike-through of some of the resin is not too noticeable with acrylics. Pile fabrics and rugs are back-coated with acrylics; they serve to bind the fibers and lengthen the life of the product. These treatments will not deteriorate for the life of the fabric as will rubber back-coating treatments. On automobile upholstery the staining by grease and oil and the effect of sun and rain will rapidly destroy the appearance of rubber back-coated products. Acrylics eliminate these problems, but are somewhat more costly. The acrylic bath used for back-coating may be used alone, or compounded with clays and fillers.

The rapidly growing field of nonwoven fabrics uses a fair amount of acrylic resins in its production as bonding agents. They are used for interlinings to resist the effects of heat and perspiration, in luggage fabrics where long wear is a factor, in outerwear applications where superior weathering properties are needed, and as backings for reinforced plastics. In the medical field, nonwoven swabs and gauzes that are subjected to steam sterilization use acrylic resins as the binder, as they will take the steam treatment without deteriorating or yellowing.

Solution polymers are used as base and top coatings for textiles and other plastic films. They adhere well to many synthetic and natural fibers and serve to bind and waterproof the fabric. Application can be by coating, dipping or spray gun. The softer acrylates are more difficult to spray because of their tendency to string. Although usually used alone, the acrylic solution may be compounded with other film formers such as polyvinyl chloride, nitrocellulose, and chorinated rubber to alter their properties.

Paper

The use of paper and paper products has enjoyed phenomenal growth within recent years. Many products that had been traditionally made of wood, fabric and even ceramics and steel are now made of paper. Many of the present uses of paper would not have been possible without the development of the synthetic resins with which they are treated.

The natural materials used in the coating of paper and paperboard have been casein and starch. The advent of synthetics and evaluation of their properties for paper progressed rapidly and at present, they have in part replaced the natural materials, and in some instances replaced them entirely.

Over the broad field, the synthetics are still used in combination with the natural binders and are usually the smaller part of the binder formulation. Synthetic rubber latices have found extensive uses for coating paper. Acrylics have had use in smaller volume for specialty items. Their excellent properties have always interested the paper manufacturer, and the single factor of cost has been the biggest deterrent to more widespread use. Introduction of higher solids emulsions and lowering of resin manufacturing costs have stimulated acrylic paper-coating activity. The introduction of paper cartons and paper drums where outdoor weathering and moisture resistance became important further increased the interest in acrylics. It is anticipated that growth in this field will continue.

The synthetic used for paper coating is required to perform a number of basic functions. It must bind the clay and the pigment with which it is compounded; it must bond the entire mix to the paper substrate, and it must be able to accept ink without cracking or picking from a high-speed printing process. In addition, it should be mechanically and chemically stable in the coating bath, add strength to the paper, level and dry quickly and easily, have high gloss, water resistance and low residual odor. The coated paper can have no tackiness or blocking characteristics even at somewhat elevated temperature. Crocking should be at a minimum.

Acrylic resins have been developed that fit these requirements fairly well. The mechanical stability of these emulsions is sufficient to allow the bath to be pumped and handled on the roll, brush and knife blade coaters used in paper coating. The water resistance after complete drying is good, and absence of residual odor is proved by the fact that acrylic-treated papers have been used for food wrapping. All acrylic systems have good gloss properties and can be calendered to a high gloss if compounded properly. The clarity of the acrylic film is of value in producing colored coatings of high brilliance.

Typical formulations for paper contain about 6 to 8 per cent acrylic resin solids to about 85 per cent clay. The balance may be various proteins and pigments. These formulations will vary for different coaters and different paper stocks. These are, of course, high acrylic polymer formulations and as the amount of acrylic is lessened, the amount of protein or casein is increased. Addition to the formulation of antiblocking agents may be needed. Talc is often used and a portion of a wax emulsion. The bath is made alkaline with small amounts of ammonia. Manufacturers of acrylic emulsions have made available many suggested formulations for paper coating baths. There is considerable variation from one to the other. The experienced paper coater will find formulation not too difficult when his knowledge is applied to a specific resin.

The use of solution polymers in the paper treating field is of lesser interest. They have been used as saturants rather than coatings for the making of specialty papers. There are also cases where they have been used to both saturate and laminate paper.

Emulsion Paints

The story of emulsion-based paints is a fast-moving tale of the quick success afforded to the resin product that builds the better mousetrap. Fifteen years ago practically all the paint used was based on various oil formulations. Just after World War II the first real success was achieved with the introduction of water emulsion paints based on a butadiene-styrene polymer in emulsion form. These were referred to as rubber-base paints, and quickly appealed to the "do-it-yourself" market because they were easy to apply. The paint film had the usual disadvantages associated with rubber. It was embrittled on aging and was subject to discoloration. The latices had poor freeze resistance and emulsion breakage was not unusual. Changes in the polymer caused poor shelf life and viscosity build-up in storage. Changes were needed to improve the system, both in the polymer used and the additives.

Rubber-base paints were followed very soon by the polyvinyl acetate emulsions and improved formulations. Volume of paint produced grew rapidly and cut sharply into the oil paint market. Two years ago it was estimated that about half of the interior paint used was based on emulsion vehicles. By now this percentage has been exceeded.

Acrylic emulsion paints entered the field six years ago and were found to be superior for interior use to the products on the market in a number of respects. They exhibited better scrub resistance and would not yellow on aging. Storage stability was excellent and they were highly resistant to freezing. They dried very rapidly and a second coat could be applied within about an hour. The odor on drying was negligible and normal ventilation was adequate during painting. It was also found that acrylic paints could be applied over damp surfaces and over plaster and cement products without any adverse effect.

The introduction of the acrylic paints with their improved properties began to interest the commercial painting contractors, and they are widely used today for commercial and institutional painting in spite of a higher price than other products. The ease of handling and the ability to put on two coats without moving the scaffold resulted in a labor saving that balanced the higher cost.

Testing of a paint is a long and tedious process. Many of the usual film tests and emulsion tests apply, and these are easily performed; many accelerated aging tests indicate a good product. But the real test is to apply the paint to many structures in many climates and then simply wait until the paint fails in use. For an exterior paint, this may take five years or more—and the entire acrylic paint program is only six years old. The tests to date have been so satisfactory that almost a dozen emulsion producers have entered the field in the last years with both acrylic and vinyl-acrylic copolymers.

The acrylic emulsion for paint purposes is a three-component polymer of ethyl acrylate, methyl methacrylate and methacrylic acid. There is variation from product to product in the ratio but the ethyl acrylate is present in major proportion and the acid component is present in a few per cent or less. Emulsion solids are available from about 48 to 55 per cent.

Each emulsion manufacturer suggests paint formulations that have been tried with his product. These formulations

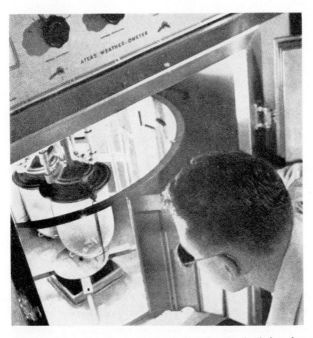

Acrylic emulsion paints have proved their value for both interior and exterior use. Accelerated testing in a Weather-O-Meter helps to indicate which paints will best stand the test of time. (*Courtesy of The Rohm & Haas Reporter,* **16**, *#5, September-October 1958.*)

are to be considered as starting points for the paint manufacturer and he will make many substitutions and changes in amounts before he is satisfied with his product. The paint formulation consists of eight functional ingredients: pigment, filler or extender, wetting and dispersing agent, preservative, anti-foaming agent, thickener, corrosion inhibitor, and binder. In addition the use of a leveling agent is desirable.

The following formulation is suggested by one manufacturer of emulsions as a semi gloss exterior white:

	Parts by Weight
Rutile titanium dioxide	36.00
Lithopone	27.00
Micro-mica	9.00
Sodium benzoate	0.63
Sodium pentachlorphenate	0.06
Sodium tripolyphosphate	0.36
Diethylene glycol	1.00
Water	26.00
	100.05

This pigment phase is dispersed by a three-roll or ball mill. The pigment dispersion is then made into a paint by mixing in a change can mixer with emulsion and water:

	% by Weight
Pigment paste	50.3
Acrylic emulsion	36.7
Water	13.0

Total solids in the formulation is 54.4 per cent and the pigment to binder ratio is 200/100. For indoor use the pigment paste binder ratio can be increased to as high as 500/100.

Industrial baking finishes based on the use of acrylic emulsion binders have been used for prime and topcoats on metal substrates. The acrylic emulsion is a cross-linkable type which forms a very tough and adherent film when baked. Comparison of this system to a standard alkyd enamel showed that the acrylic had equivalent properties in many respects, and had superior adhesion, flexibility and impact strength.

Lacquers of excellent quality are made with acrylic solution polymers. Alone or in combination with other synthetics they are formulated into nonyellowing white lacquers for metal surfaces that will resist discoloration at very high temperatures. For modern furniture woods of light color where water-white, age-resisting lacquers are desirable, acrylic-based materials are the best choice. In 1958, 35 per cent of the passenger cars made by General Motors used methacrylate lacquer for surface coatings, and it is expected that this will increase to 100 per cent. Manufacturers of kitchen equipment and appliances use acrylic synthetics for protective and decorative coatings that will remain substantially unchanged for the life of the product.

Polymer Floor Waxes

A fairly recent innovation is the use of emulsion polymers in the compounding of modern floor waxes for industrial and household purposes. The requirements of such a product are many. It must be easy to apply and level and dry quickly. It must have a high gloss but not be slippery. It must resist the scuffing of feet and adhere well to the floor. Accidentally spilled water or other liquids should not penetrate or stain the surface but removal with water and soap or detergent should be rapid. Very fine particle resin emulsions in combination with wax emulsions and water-soluble alkyd resins or polyethylene emulsions are now in wide use. The first resin emulsions used were based on polystyrene, but acrylics followed rapidly and many products are now based on acrylics or combinations of styrene and acrylics. The emulsion film for this purpose must be clear, glossy, and hard, but still tough and flexible. The acrylics add the non-yellowing feature, as opposed to styrene.

The acrylic monomers used in floor waxes are methyl methacrylate, methyl acrylate and ethyl acrylate, methacrylic acid and in some cases, acrylonitrile. The emulsion is usually just on the verge of being film-forming, and with the plasticizing effect of the other ingredients in the formulation, it will form a hard film.

There is no optimum product on the market today that solves all the floor waxing problems, but the synthetics are highly superior to the old natural resin and wax combinations. Much laboratory work is being done to improve the products and it is to be expected that better products will evolve. Formulations available include both the buffable and self-polishing varieties. Acrylics that are useful in floor wax compounding have also found use in the formulation of shoe polishes and shoe dressings in combination with natural or synthetic waxes.

Leather Base Coating

For the base coating of leather, acrylic emulsions are used almost exclusively. The emulsion serves as a binder for the pigment and forms a strong bond with the surface of the tanned hide. It must also form a strong but flexible film that will not harden and crack on aging. The softer polymers of the lower acrylic esters are used for the leathers destined for garment use, and somewhat harder films are used for heavier leathers. The basic formulation for leather priming consists of a diluted mix of acrylic emulsion and pigment dispersion. The pigment binder ratio will vary, depending on how much it is desired to mask the leather grain. To the bath may be added a preservative, and casein may be used to make a harder film and reduce residual tackiness. It does lessen the flexibility of the film. A higher ratio of pigment to binder will improve the pore-filling properties of the paint and its rub resistance but it also reduces the flexibility of the film.

Absorption into the skin is a function of the amount of water in the mix and the type of surfactant used in the

The hand application of acrylic emulsions to fine leather surfaces is a familiar sight in the leather finishing plant. After the base coat has dried, a lacquer topcoat will be sprayed on. (*Courtesy of The Rohm & Haas Reporter, August 1959.*)

emulsion preparation. Too much "sink in" is undesirable because it decreases the hiding power of the pigment; too little may affect adhesion adversely and give the leather an overpainted effect. If the leather is greasy, addition of alcohol to the bath will assist the penetration. A minor percentage of wax emulsion in the bath will improve the wet rub properties, reduce tack and prevent sticking in hot embossing.

The base coating of leather is one of the cases where a small degree of cross-linking of polymer is highly advantageous. High strength in flexing and stretching is required, and yet the coating must be soft. A minor amount of cross-linking will not appreciably harden the polymer film but its toughness and elasticity will be markedly increased. The use of a small amount of a divalent metal salt that will link through acid groups in the polymer chain is one of the suggested methods. Other efficient cross-linking methods are also being used. Cross-linked resins will also show improved resistance to cracking in cold weather.

Acrylic Adhesives

The acrylate monomers and polymers are used for a wide range of adhesive products. Depending on the choice of acrylic used, the adhesives will range from pressure-sensitives to hard, fused bonds. Their ability to withstand time, weathering and heat without change make them useful for permanent bonds, and their clarity makes them specific where the bonded materials are transparent and the adhesive is visible.

Monomers with a little catalyst can be polymerized *in situ* to form excellent bonds. Plastic sheets (including cast acrylic sheets) are frequently bonded in this way. The solvent property of the monomer first softens the surface of the plastic to be bonded and then, on polymerization, forms a strong invisible bond. Monomer-polymer mixture may also be used in place of monomer alone.

A recent newcomer to the acrylic adhesives is a solventless monomer, alpha-cyanoacrylate. It will polymerize at room temperature without catalyst or hardener. It has been shown to develop very high bond strength with glass and rubber, and shear values of as high as 4500 psi are attainable with metal surfaces. It is too high in cost for any but the most unusual bonding problems and small traces of acid lower

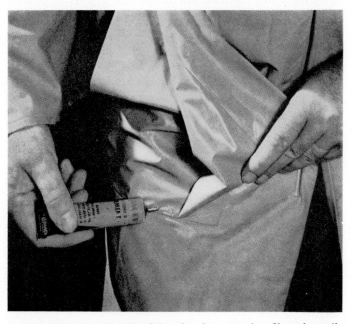

Household cement in collapsible tubes has spread a film of acrylic solution polymer into every nook and cranny. (*Courtesy of The Rohm & Haas Reporter,* **16,** *#4, July-August 1958.*)

the bond strength. It is, however, an unusual bonding material and may indicate future directions in high bonding strength materials.

Polymer adhesives operate by three different systems. The air-dry or solvent release method may be based on either solution polymers or water emulsions. The monomers used may produce polymers that are soft and flexible, tough and elastic, or hard and brittle depending on the application. In using this method the adhesive is allowed to dry partially and then the surfaces to be bonded are pressed together. It is desirable that at least one of the surfaces to be bonded be porous to allow the solvent to evaporate completely. The use of heat will speed the process.

Another method that does not have the problems of solvent evaporation is the hot-melt process. Solid powdered or granular polymers are spread between the surfaces to be bonded and the assembly is placed in a hot press. The heat causes the polymer to melt and flow, and a strong bond results. The harder polymers based on methyl and ethyl methacrylate are used for this purpose.

The third bonding system is the pressure-sensitive adhesive. This is based on the lower acrylic esters that normally retain their high tack when dry. Ethyl acrylate, butyl acrylate and 2-ethyl-hexyl acrylate are commonly employed in pressure-sensitive adhesive formulations. Styrene, vinyl acetate or vinyl ethers are frequently copolymerized with the acrylates for this type of product. Pressure-sensitive adhesives are available that have good adhesion and cohesion on initial contact; on heating or aging they develop much higher bond strength through built-in cross-linking systems.

Acrylic emulsions are also available for the bonding of glass mat preforms used in the manufacture of reinforced plastics. This acrylic will withstand the temperatures of cure without discoloring, and will adhere well to glass fibers.

9. MISCELLANEOUS ACRYLIC MONOMERS AND APPLICATIONS

The preceding chapter dealt primarily with acrylic ester resins and some of their major uses. There still remain to be discussed other uses for acrylic esters and a number of other acrylic monomers and their resins. Although brought together under a miscellaneous heading, the products to be described are far from small in volume of sales. One of the products, acrylonitrile rubber, is a major elastomer and could well deserve a complete book of its own.

WATER-SOLUBLE POLYMERS

A number of acrylic polymers are water-soluble compounds that have found wide use as industrial materials. Polymers made from acrylic and methacrylic acids and their sodium and ammonium salts are foremost in this group. Polyacrylamide is a new water-soluble gum made by the polymerization of acrylamide and offered in various ranges of molecular weights. Other water-soluble and gel-forming acrylics include polymers of methacrylamide, N-methylolacrylamide, hydroxyethyl acrylates, and N,N'-methylenebisacrylamide.

Polymerization of these monomers is carried out in a water medium using a persulfate or redox catalyst system. Acrylic and methacrylic acid and their salts polymerize quite readily. The product is a quite viscous solution or a gel depending on the concentration of the polymer and the degree of polymerization. Polymerization carried out at higher temperatures yields more soluble products of lower molecular weight. The

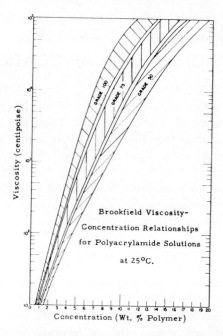

Brookfield Viscosity-
Concentration Relationships
for Polyacrylamide Solutions
at 25°C.

Polymers of acrylic acid and salts have proved their value as industrial thickeners. Polyacrylamide, a relative newcomer, is also efficient for this purpose. The chart shows the thickening action of three grades of polyacrylamide of varying molecular weight. (*Reproduced from Tappi,* **40,** *#9, Sept. 1957.*)

polymers of acrylic acid and salts are sold in water solution. Methacrylic acid is usually sold as a dry product as are the higher molecular weight polyacrylamides.

The homopolymers of acrylic and methacrylic acid cannot be used for the conventional purposes as the acrylic esters because of their water solubility. They are brittle when dry and are not thermoplastic but cross-link on heating. At high temperatures they decompose without softening. They are useful in the textile trade as sizes for yarn and are particularly applied to nylon yarns. Some use has been made of polyacrylic acid as an emulsion suspension agent. Methacrylic acid polymers that have been cross-linked with a difunctional product, such as divinylbenzene, are used as cation exchange resins. Interesting medical uses have been found for this resin in the reduction of edema caused by high salt content in the body. In the pharmaceutical field, this type of resin has been used to recover antibiotics during their manufacture.

The sodium and ammonium salts of acrylic and methacrylic acid yield polymers that are used as thickeners of natural and synthetic latices for dipping, casting and adhesive compositions, for pigments and printing pastes, and as protective colloids and emulsifying agents. In the granular polymerization of methyl methacrylate and styrene they are used as granulating agents. Cross-linked polymers of methacrylic acid have been carefully studied; it has been observed that a change of pH from acid to base and back to acid again causes a contraction and dilation of the polymer chain that resembles the action of muscle fibers.

Polyacrylamide has recently been introduced as a synthetic, water-soluble gum. It is available in a number of degrees of polymerization. The lowest molecular weight product is sold as a water solution and those of higher molecular weight are available as dry, water soluble granules. Acrylamide presented polymerization problems in terms of reproducibility in the range desired and these had to be overcome before a standard product could be offered for use. The polymers can be used for flocculation, dispersion, thickening, adhesion and to form films or gels.

Methylated and methylolated derivatives of polyacrylamide have been suggested for various uses. Paper sizing properties and wet strength potential have been evaluated. Polyacrylamide has possible uses as a soil additive for erosion prevention, coatings for rubber products, thickening agent in latex paints, and various textile uses.

ACRYLONITRILE AND ACRYLIC RUBBER

This versatile and least expensive acrylic monomer is widely used in its polymeric form for a variety of purposes. As a copolymer with butadiene it forms highly superior synthetic rubber. Copolymerized with a portion of vinyl chloride or vinyl acetate, it can be drawn into fibers that are widely used for the newest synthetic fabrics. This subject will be considered separately. It is often used with the acrylic ester polymers to add strength and toughness. These and many other uses have made this an important member of the acrylic family. It can be polymerized by the usual bulk, solution or emulsion methods and copolymerizes readily with other members of the vinyl monomer grouping.

Synthetic rubber is essentially a copolymer of styrene and butadiene. It was found that the substitution, in whole or in part, of acrylonitrile for the styrene produced a rubber which overcame many of the problems inherent in the styrene product. Copolymerization is done by emulsion techniques under redox conditions to produce the rubber latex. For use in coatings and impregnations the latex is the finished product. The emulsion is coagulated to produce slab rubber by precipitating with a salt solution, followed by washing and drying of the crumb. The dry crumb is then compounded and milled into the slab.

In the selection of the best elastomer for a specific purpose it is necessary to weigh the advantages of one against the other and find the best possible compromise. Acrylonitrile-butadiene rubber is inherently oil- and solvent-resistant. These properties increase with the acrylonitrile content of the polymer, and there is also an increase in the toughness, tensile strength and hardness. As the acrylonitrile content decreases the product becomes more soluble and more resilient. Its low-temperature impact strength also improves. The cost of the rubber is also dependent on the amount of acrylonitrile, which is the more expensive ingredient. The problems involved in this compromise procedure have also led to the wide use of ABS rubber, a tripolymer of acrylonitrile-butadiene-styrene which has properties that are midway between GR-S and acrylonitrile rubber.

Acrylonitrile rubber has low permeability to gases and better resistance to many chemicals than ordinary rubber. It has higher than ordinary heat resistance and, although affected by aging, has a much longer useful life. Resistance to creep and to abrasion is good, and machinability is fair. Like other rubber it will darken on aging but not as rapidly, and its original color is very light.

In the latex form, acrylonitrile rubber is used in the preparation of cements, dipped goods, coating and saturants. Products include such items as tarpaulins, electrical tape, coated metal products and work gloves. It is also used for bonding of nonwoven fabrics and in making various specialty papers. Caulking compounds and gasketing materials are also latex products. Extrusion of molding granules produces hose suitable for gasoline and oil. Injection and compression moldings produce a broad variety of standard mechanical items.

Acrylonitrile polymerized with vinylidene chloride or ethyl acrylate produces good quality paint films and with styrenated alkyds makes an excellent air-dry lacquer that can be baked to give a hard and chemically inert finish. Newer reinforced

EIGHT ACRYLONITRILE-BUTADIENE EMULSION POLYMERS AND THEIR SUGGESTED USES. (Goodyear Rubber "Chemigum")

Polymer type and Monomer ratio	Butadiene-acrylonitrile 55/45	Butadiene-acrylonitrile 55/45	Butadiene-acrylonitrile 67/33	Butadiene-acrylonitrile 67/33	Butadiene-acrylonitrile 67/33	Butadiene-acrylonitrile 67/33	Butadiene-acrylonitrile 67/33	Butadiene-acrylonitrile 70/30
Total Solids, %	42.5	40	32.5	42.5	40	42.5	55	55
Stabilizer	Synthetic anionic	Special soap	Synthetic anionic (minimum stabilization)	Synthetic anionic	Special soap	Synthetic anionic	Synthetic anionic	Ammonium soap
Antioxidant	Non-staining	Non-staining	Non-staining	Non-staining	Non-staining	Non-staining	Non-staining	Non-staining
pH	9.0	10.0	11.0	9.0	10.0	9.0	9.0	10.5
Average particle size, ångstroms	2500	500	1500	2500	500	2000	2500	4000
Specific gravity of latex solids	0.99	0.99	0.98	0.98	0.98	0.98	0.98	0.98
Solids, lb/gal	3.5	3.3	2.7	3.5	3.3	3.5	4.5	4.5
Latex, lb/gal	8.3	8.3	8.2	8.2	8.2	8.2	8.2	8.2
Viscosity, cps	20	80	15	20	100	20	200	100

Surface tension, dynes/cm	34	42	57	37	46	30	35	34
Mechanical stability	Excellent	Excellent	Fair	Excellent	Excellent	Excellent	Excellent	Good
Storage stability	Excellent	Very good	Very good	Excellent	Very good	Excellent	Excellent	Good
Acid and salt ion tolerance	High	Low	Low	High	Low	Average	Medium	Low
Film properties	Rubbery	Rubbery	Rubbery	Rubbery	Rubbery	Rubbery	Rubbery	Rubbery, very slightly tacky
Uses	Non-woven fabrics Textile inks Leather treatment	Beater impregnation of paper Leather finishing Textile inks Saturation of paper Leather treatment	Beater impregnation of paper	Carpet-backing compounds Paper coatings Textile coatings	Beater impregnation of paper Paper coatings Paper saturation	Carpet-backing compounds Paper coatings Textile coatings	Carpet-backing compounds Adhesives Fabric coatings	Adhesives Asphalt modifier

plastics based on acrylonitrile and polyolefins are entering the field in competition with polyesters. Rubber-phenolic resins are used for bonding in the shoe industry. Acrylonitrile rubber has good properties for this purpose.

Several types of acrylic rubbers have been made that are based on acrylic esters rather than acrylonitrile. The major component in such a system is ethyl acrylate. These are vulcanizable and have some excellent properties. It should be understood that the term "vulcanize" in connection with acrylic rubbers does not necessarily mean the traditional sulfur vulcanizing that is used for natural rubber. In this case the term means the toughening of the rubber by cross-linking. Various cross-linking systems are used, e.g., sulfur and accelerators, amines, dioximes, metal oxides, and dinitrobenzene.

"Lactoprene EV" is one of a series of ethyl acrylate rubbers developed by the Eastern Regional Laboratory, U.S. Department of Agriculture. It is now made commercially. It has been prepared by emulsion polymerization, using ammonium persulfate as the catalyst and an anionic emulsifier. It has also been prepared by granulation polymerization in a heavy-duty sigma blade mixer without the use of an emulsifier and is obtained as a fluffy granular polymer ready for baling or compounding. The formulation for this product is 95 per cent ethyl acrylate and 5 per cent alpha-chloroethyl vinyl ether. The product is superior to standard rubbers with respect to flex life, oil resistance, and heat and aging degradation. Its low-temperature properties are somewhat deficient. Another product, "Lactoprene BN," performs more efficiently at low temperatures and also has better heat and oil resistance.

EMBEDMENTS IN METHACRYLATE RESINS

Several years ago there appeared on store counters a group of attractive items of a decorative nature. They consisted of a shapely block of crystal clear plastic with various objects embedded in the center of the block. Insects, fishing flies, flowers, etc. were some of the objects in the plastic and the product could be used as a paper weight, or just a decoration. The plastic used for the embedment was cast polymeric methyl methacrylate. The commercial product was an outcome of work done in scientific laboratories to preserve specimens and still allow them to be easily viewed. Museums are now using this process for delicate objects. Another use for the embedded specimen is to permit thin sections of an object of interest to be cut for microscopic viewing and the preparation of permanent slides for teaching demonstrations.

The making of embedments is fairly simple in technique, although skill is needed in the preparation of the specimen. The object to be embedded is placed on a piece of cast sheet in a dish and a pre-polymer syrup is poured over it. Polymerization of the syrup in thin sections can build the polymer into a heavy block. Sheets of tightly fitted cellophane are used to exclude the air. The cast block is then machined and polished to optically clear surfaces.

OIL ADDITIVES

Petroleum oils used for lubrication and fuels present, in use, a number of chemical and physical problems. Many of these problems have been alleviated or overcome by the use of a variety of chemical oil additives. Acrylic polymers have been found to be very effective and large amounts of higher methacrylates are now being used for the purpose.

One of the problems in the use of lubricating oil for automobile engines is pointed up by the difficulties of starting a cold car in the winter and in the need for having winter and summer oils of different viscosities. A typical naphthenic base oil may vary in viscosity by a ratio of almost 1000 to 1 from a cold winter start to the 180°F running temperature. Starting puts a strain on the battery and, at running temperature, the oil may be too thin to lubricate adequately. The incorporation of low molecular weight polymers of higher methacrylate esters in small percentages improves this viscosity index markedly.

The waxes naturally present in oils cause a rapid thickening of the oil as the temperature is reduced. Dewaxing by extraction is resorted to in order to depress this pour-point temperature. In some crudes the use of these methacrylic polymers serves to depress the pour point without the need for wax extraction. Hydraulic fluids for aircraft are also used with acrylic additives to improve their efficiency.

Amyl, octyl, lauryl and cetyl methacrylates are polymerized for oil additives in the presence of benzoyl peroxide. They are supplied as viscous solutions in oil for convenient addition. Recent patents indicate that the addition of monomers of methacrylanilide and beta-diethylaminoethyl methacrylate as a minor copolymerizing constituent gives a product that will prevent the formation of crankcase sludge and deposition of varnish-like gums. Another patent claims an improved product by the use of a portion of vinyl pyridine. Oleyl methacrylate has also been proposed as an oil additive.

Fuel oils used for heating are liable to deteriorate in storage. This is particularly true of fuel oils made by catalytic cracking. Oxidation during storage causes the deposition of a sludge that clogs filters and nozzles. Here again the addition of polymers based on technical "Lorol" methacrylate copolymerized with a nitrogen bearing methacrylate helps to alleviate the problem.

ACRYLIC FIBERS

The never-ending search by man for better clothing is almost as old as the story of man himself, and is only secondary to the search for food. The spinning and weaving of natural fibers into cloth is an ancient art and one of the basic essentials of civilization. It was only natural that the growth of technology should include simultaneous growth in an understanding of fibers and attempts to improve on the natural products. As long ago as 1664, Sidney Hooke predicted the use of artificial fibers when he understood that it should be possible to transform non-fibrous materials into fiber form. More than 200 years after this prediction rayon fibers were produced in 1884. From this time on the growth of the synthetic fiber industry has been rapid. At present, new fibers, like new cars, are a yearly occurrence.

Acrylic fibers are a comparative newcomer on the scene. The first research was started in the early 1940's by DuPont when investigation was started into the possible use of polyacrylonitrile as a fiber. Success came rapidly, and there are ten acrylic fibers listed at the present time. "Orlon," "Acrilan," "Dynel," and "Creslan" have become household words and production is measured in many hundreds of tons. All this has happened in less than twenty years.

The making of fibers starts with the production of high molecular weight polymer. This polymer is then put into a semi-liquid form by either melting or dissolving in a suitable solvent. The melt or viscous solution is then extruded through a die with very fine holes into a long fiber. The fiber is still an amorphous plastic that is much too weak and must still be oriented before it is useful. Mention has been made previously of the biaxial stretching of cast sheet to add strength to the product and to the orienting of films to make them tough. The stretching process serves to straighten out the tangle of polymer chains and to add a degree of crystallinity to their structure. The extruded fiber is also oriented by stretching lengthwise with an accompanying loss in thickness and very high increase in tensile strength. The fiber is then ready to be spun, felted, or used as a monofilament.

The strength of fibers is measured in grams per denier. This is the weight that will break a fiber of a certain diameter. Denier is the total weight in grams of 9000 meters of the filament or yarn. The creep, elasticity, deformation under load, and recovery are all factors that are used in determining the value of a fiber. Water resistance, chemical stability, and properties of aging are all of great importance.

As would be expected, it is in the field of resistance to aging and sunlight that the acrylic fibers are outstanding. Fibers of acrylics also have good chemical, moisture, and heat resistance and are not subject to bacterial attack.

Fibers of 100 per cent acrylonitrile are difficult to dye. Its chemical inertness is the basis for the dyeing problem, although this inert quality is one of its good features. To overcome this dyeing problem many modified fibers have been tried. To date dyeability has been greatly improved, but the task is far from finished. Opening of the fiber to facilitate diffusion of the dye, use of anionic dye receptors, copolymerizing the acrylonitrile with other polymers, and care in choice of dye and method of application have all added up to the partial solution of the problem.

"Acrilan" is an acrylonitrile fiber that has been copolymerized with other materials to promote dyeability. The polymer is dissolved in gamma-valerolactone, a high-boiling solvent, and wet-spun to form continuous strands. The strand is washed, stretched, crimped and cut into staple. The product has good resistance to mineral acids and organic solvents and is unaffected by moths and mildew. It has high wrinkle resistance and thermo-insulation properties similar to wool. The warm hand and bulky nature of the fiber make it useful for blankets, outdoor fabrics and linings.

A copolymer of 60 per cent vinyl chloride and 40 per cent

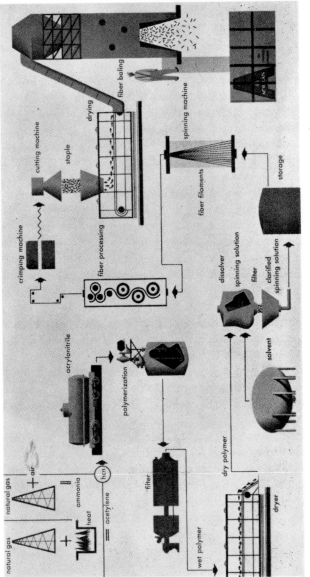

Flow sheet for the manufacture of a typical acrylonitrile textile fiber. (*Courtesy of The Chemstrand Corp.*)

acrylonitrile is called "Dynel." The polymer is dissolved in acetone and run through the spinneret into a spinning bath. This is followed by drying, stretching, cutting and crimping into the staple. Dyeing is done by the use of swelling agents and acid dyes. Men's hosiery, pile fabrics, blankets and fleece linings are some of the uses of "Dynel," and it also finds use in combination with other fibers, both natural and synthetic. These combinations have been useful for suitings, underwear, skirts, and dresses.

The first and best known of the acrylic fibers is "Orlon." This is made by polymerizing acrylonitrile, dissolving in dimethyl formamide, filtering and extruding through the spinneret. It is dried and stretched and then either left in monofilament form or cut to make staple fiber for spinning. Its strength and recovery are excellent and long exposure to heat below 300°F has little effect. Monofilaments retained full strength when subjected to 257°F for one month. The original "Orlon" had great chemical inertness and was difficult to dye, but more recent variations of the product have been offered that show good dyeability and fastness. Many types of garments are made of "Orlon" that are light in weight, easily laundered and wrinkle-resistant. A large use is in the field of industrial fabrics such as work clothes and filter cloths, and for outdoor fabrics such as auto tops, lawn umbrellas and awnings.

A new and versatile acrylonitrile fiber is known as "Creslan." It is recommended for use in fabrics ranging all the way from conventional alpacas or gabardines to knitted sweaters. Other names of acrylic fibers are "Acrylast," which is produced as a filament, and "Verel" which is a staple. Acrylic fibers have been used to make excellent imitations of fur and more and more industrial uses are being found including the making of acrylic rope.

10. FUTURE TRENDS

Almost sixty years have passed since the beginnings of the development of acrylics as a useful material. Only the last twenty-five of these have been devoted to industrial growth. In retrospect, those who have worked in the field can feel justly proud that they have helped nurse the baby to its present stage. Those who are engaged in day-to-day work with acrylics still feel that it is indeed a baby, and a lusty one. They are aware of its past history but are fully involved with its future. And they are convinced that this future will be a lively one. It is difficult to be unimpressed with the myriad of applications to which acrylics have been adapted and to the rapidity with which new potential is being discovered. Competition with other plastics is severe, as it should be, but the acrylic chemist feels that he has a better product wherever quality is involved.

MONOMER COST FACTORS

Since acrylics always seem to cost just a little more, some understanding of this factor is in order. It is true that some of the raw materials used in the manufacture of the monomers are not natural materials, as in the case of polyethylene and other plastics, but are manufactured intermediates that must necessarily be more costly. It is also within the realm of the very possible that better methods of producing the monomers, using lower cost materials and processing methods, will be developed. There are now two producers of methacrylic esters in the United States. If a third producer should enter the field, there is every possibility that prices will become lower.

Plant for producing acrylic esters. (*Courtesy of Union Carbide Chemicals Co.*)

Hawthorne Chemical Co., a subsidiary of Hercules Powder Co., almost took the giant step a few years ago. They announced plans for a methacrylate plant using Imperial Chemical Industries know-how. At the last minute, plans were dropped for no specific reason. It should be noted at this point that the two present suppliers of methacrylates use a large portion of their production for captive purposes. Both DuPont and Rohm & Haas are in competition with their own mono-mer customers. The recent announcement by Dow Chemical Co. of its styrene-methacrylate molding powder indicates that it may have a methacrylate plant in mind. Other companies are also known to be investigating the possibility.

Acrylates, until recently, were the sole province of Rohm & Haas. Within the past few years, both Celanese and Union Carbide have brought acrylate plants on stream, and Dow Chemical Co. has announced that a plant is under construction. Within the past half year, the price of two of the lower acrylic esters have dropped over 25 per cent and acrylic acid in glacial form has dropped almost 50 per cent. These price decreases should cause a marked increase of acrylics in the field of softer coatings and pressure-sensitive adhesives. It is assumed that part of the market gained would be at the expense of vinyl acetate and rubber latices.

POLYMER PRODUCTION FIGURES

Compilation of gross figures for the industry is a difficult problem, as those that are available are only reasonably reliable educated guesses. In 1956, an interested company compiled a projected figure for methacrylate sales in 1960 based on sales in 1955. Their projection showed a gross sale in 1960 of 125,000,000 pounds of methacrylates. The rapid growth due to new developments is indicated by the fact that the 125,000,000 figure was reached in 1958, two years sooner than the projection showed.

Breakdown of the gross figure for methacrylates in 1958 indicates that about 28,000,000 pounds were used in the form of molding powder for injection molding and extrusions. Extrusions can account for about 5,000,000 pounds of this figure. The lighting fixture industry used about 1/4 of the extruded products. Cast products used about 1/3 of the total

or about 40,000,000 pounds. Aircraft use has been going
down, but use in signs, glazing, and architectural uses is increasing. From 17 to 20,000,000 pounds were used in polymeric lauryl methacrylate for oil additives. Emulsions and
solutions for coatings make up the balance sold. These were
used for automobile lacquers and other decorative and protective coatings and impregnations.

Figures for production of acrylates are almost unattainable.
Gross figures for specific products using acrylic esters have
been published. About 8,000,000 gallons of acrylic emulsion
paint were sold in 1958 and 500,000,000 pounds of acrylic
elastomers. An export figure for 1958 that includes both
acrylate and methacrylate totals 12,000,000 pounds.

FUTURE POSSIBILITIES FOR SOLID ACRYLIC RESINS

The search for improvement in cast products continues at a
lively pace. Production methods are still based on the gasketed
glass cell that is filled and handled one at a time. Labor cost is
high for the operation, production is slow, and stocking of the
many sizes, shapes and colors represents a large investment.
A number of patents have been issued describing continuous
and semi-continuous sheet production, but these have not
generally been used because the product has proved inferior.
The field is still wide open for a continuous method of casting.
Extruded sheet has been improving in quality and is put to
use, where possible, in place of cast sheet. Further improvements in extrusions are needed to compete seriously with the
surface quality and properties of the cast product.

Two of the faults of castings have been solved by the use
of copolymer products and partial cross-linking. The heat
resistance has been raised to the point where special castings
are boilable and surface crazing has been reduced to a minimum. The J. T. Baker Co. has recently announced a new

acrylic molding and extrusion powder that has a heat-distortion temperature of 250°F, and the Glasflex Corporation claims a line of cast sheet and rod with heat distortion of 240°F and high resistance to crazing. It is still formable at elevated temperatures. The problem of surface scratching is still to be solved. All attempts in this direction have failed. "Gafite" was an excellent product for this reason, but the price was excessive. Copolymers that are scratch-resistant tend to lose thermoplasticity, and cannot be readily formed. This field is still wide open for the future inventor and the reward will be great.

Recent announcements of new uses for cast acrylics have been appearing at a rapid rate. Cast Optics now offer blocks from 6 to 24 inches thick. These blocks are supplied with two parallel surfaces polished and to dimension. One of the uses for these blocks is for the viewing of radioactive materials. Glasflex and Cast Optics produce high quality cast rod used in the manufacture of contact lenses. Acrylic parts are used in the blood oxygenator for open heart surgery. Model makers use combinations of cast acrylics and aluminum for scale models of new buildings. Acrylic pistons, worms and other machine parts are used for food production and for handling corrosive materials. Acrylic colored chips have invaded the mosaic field and are used for many decorative objects. A line of occasional tables uses a free form acrylic mosaic pattern that is bonded with a polyester and then covered with a sheet of acrylic. The surface is durable and stain-resistant. A novel automobile sun visor of transparent blue acrylic has been offered as a replacement for the present product. It will eliminate sun and road glare, is transparent and will not block the driver's view.

An answer to improved properties in acrylic extrusions has been offered by DuPont's "Lucite 147." Sheet extruded with this material is reported to be of high optical level and has higher resistance to crazing caused by solvents and cleaning agents used in maintenance of finished products. The resin is recommended for use in the sign and lighting industry. It is also suggested for a new application as trim and moldings for autos, boats, and buildings.

Acrylic injection moldings have a fairly high impact strength, but for many purposes it was desirable to improve this property. A modified acrylic, "Implex" has been offered by Rohm & Haas. It has better impact resistance than the standard product and still retains the excellent general stability characteristic of acrylics. The natural color is off-white translucent and is available in a variety of opaque colors in a number of grades. It is also suggested as an improved extrusion material. It can be used to advantage on such items as women's shoe heels, business machine parts, and marine applications.

The following properties chart gives two grades of "Implex" high-impact acrylic molding compound. In addition to high impact strength, the properties include low water absorption, resistance to aging and dimensional stability.

The Dow Chemical Co. recently announced availability of a completely new copolymer molding material. It is a copolymer of methyl methacrylate and styrene and is named "Zerlon 50." Excellent properties are claimed for the product and it will be priced at about 50 cents per pound. Methacrylate molding powders are at about the 55 cent level and it is assumed that "Zerlon 50" is aimed at this market. Dow indicates that the potential of their new product will be determined by actual use in a variety of products.

REINFORCED LAMINATING RESIN

Until recently, the use of acrylics in reinforced laminates was confined to the possible addition of a little acrylic to up-

PROPERTIES OF TWO GRADES OF IMPLEX

Property	Test Conditions	"Implex A"	"Implex B"
Specific gravity	R & H P-37	1.12	1.16
Tensile strength	D638-46T (0.2"/min.)		
	Maximum, psi	5500	7300
	Modulus, psi	225,000	300,000
	% elongation (break)	>30	>25
Flexural strength	D790-49T (flatwise, 0.10"/min.)		
	Maximum, psi	8700	11500
	Modulus, psi	280,000	360,000
Impact strength	D256-47T (Method B-5" x ½" x ¼")		
	Charpy		
	at 73°F, ft-lb	30	20
	at −13°F, ft-lb	24	17
	Izod		
	at 73°, ft-lb/in. of notch	2.0	0.8
	at −13°F, ft-lb/in. of notch	0.7	0.5
Compressive strength	D695-52T (0.05"/min.)		
	Maximum, psi	7300	10,500
	Modulus, psi	250,000	325,000
Rockwell hardness	D785-51 (Method A)	L-58	L-89
Barcol hardness	R & H D-79	56	69
Heat distortion temperature	D648-45T (2°C/min.)		
	264 psi	169°F(76°C)	174°F(79°C)
	66 psi	194°F(90°C)	185°F(85°C)
Mold shrinkage	Mil/in.	4-8	4-8
Flow temperature	D569-48 Method A	320°F	295°F
Water absorption	D570-42 (24 hr immersion) weight gain, %	0.3	0.3

grade the plastic that was being used and improve its weathering properties. Early last year DuPont released information that it had available an all acrylic laminating syrup, "Lucite 201X" and "Lucite 202X." It can be used for the making of corrugated glass-reinforced sheet, flat decorative and structural sheet and other fairly complex shapes. The equipment now used in the making of polyester laminates can be adapted with small changes to run acrylic laminates. It can be fabricated by the usual molding methods of contact pressure, press lamination, or premixed with fillers to make moldings. Its curing action is similar to pre-polymer syrups used for sheets casting and must be heated to start polymerization. When the exotherm takes over, it is necessary to cool and hold at a temperature that will prevent the formation of bubbles caused by boiling of the monomer. Curing ovens for lay-ups are air-heated and air-cooled. Results will depend on efficient control of the oven temperatures. Press cures can be done in a few minutes, but control of pressures is to be done with more care than is now used in polyesters. Gradual application of pressure is desirable early in the cycle. Premix compounding of the acrylic syrup is carried out by the addition of fillers, pigments and various reinforcing fibers. The premix is cured in matched metal molds. It is claimed that costs are similar to polyesters for the finished product and less rejects are the rule. The trade is now testing this product and there are indications of some difficulty with pinholes and bubbles. It is probable that this problem will be resolved when the fabricator gains more experience in using the product.

The introduction of a monomer-polymer acrylic casting syrup opens a broad new field for acrylic applications. The chart on p. 172 gives the properties of glass-reinforced panels made from this syrup.

The experienced processor of glass laminates can see from

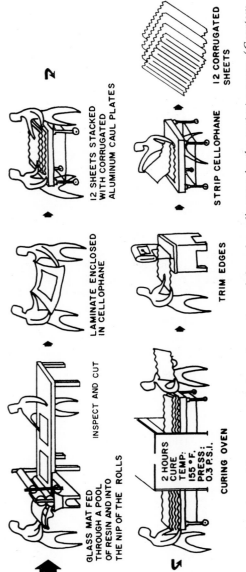

Flow chart for making corrugated sheets from glass-reinforced acrylic syrup by the contact process. (*Courtesy of Modern Plastics, August 1958.*)

Property	ASTM Test Number	Values	
Glass, % by weight	—	40	25
Method of fabrication	—	Press cure[1]	Contact cure[2]
Hardness, Rockwell "R,"	D785—51	125	121
Tensile strength, psi, 23°C	D638—56T	23,000	12,000
Elongation, %, 23°C	D638—56T	1.7	1.5
Flexural strength, psi, 23°C	D790—49T	35,000	25,000
Flexural strength, psi, 100°C	D790—49T	14,000	8,000
Flexural strength, psi, 23°C wet[3]	D790—49	30,000	—
Flexural modulus, 10^6 psi, 23°C	D790—49T	1.6	0.9
Flexural modulus, 10^6 psi, 100°C	D790—49T	0.8	0.3
Compressive strength, psi, 23°C	D695—54	25,000	24,000
Izod impact, ft-lb/in. of notch	D256—56	14	6
Taber abrasion[4]	—	30	33
Heat distortion temperature, 264 psi, °F	D648—56	256	233
Coefficient of linear thermal expansion	D696—44	4×10^{-5}	—
Flammability, in./min.	D635—56T	—	1.3
Dielectric constant, 1000 cycles	D150—54T	5.0	4.1
Dissipation factor, 1000 cycles	D150—54T	0.007	0.05
Light transmittance, total % (1/16 in.)	—	—	60-65
Diffuse transmittance, % of total	—	—	95-98

[1] Lucite 201 X.
[2] Lucite 202 X.
[3] Following 2-hr boil.
[4] Weight loss, mg/1000 cycles, CS-17, 1000 g.

the following chart of processing characteristics that his present equipment can be easily adapted to the handling of acrylic syrup.

PROCESSING CHARACTERISTICS

Molding Method	Product Line	Equipment	Cure Temperature (°F)	Cure Time (min.)	Curing Pressure (psi)
Contact pressure	Corrugated sheet	Impregnators and cure oven	155	60 to 120	0.1 to 0.3
Press lamination	Moldings and flat sheet	Press and molds	239 258	7 2 to 4	150 300 to 500
Premix	Moldings	Press and molds	258	1.5 to 3	to 1000

TRENDS IN LIQUID RESINS

If acrylic emulsions could be made in such manner that the dried film would consist of nothing but acrylic polymer, the product would eliminate many of the existing defects. But this, to date, has not been accomplished. The small amount of surfactants, salts, and residual monomer causes a weakening of the film and poorer water resistance. The ideal surfactant has not yet been found that will do its work effectively and volatilize completely on drying. Perhaps, in view of the wide uses to which emulsions have been put, this is a purist approach. But the possibility is worth a little speculation.

Despite all the work that has been done in emulsions, acrylics or otherwise, scientific understanding of the process has not reached any great heights. Much has been written about the theory involved. This theory has been useful and has permitted a degree of prediction, but emulsion making should still be classified as a refined art. The chemist whose task it is to make emulsions may not necessarily be referred to as a refined artist, but he must have a penchant for dish-washing.

At the present time stress is being put on the application of acrylic emulsion in the fields of emulsion paints, floor wax formulations, and paper coatings as large volume outlets. Other uses, although smaller in volume, also get their share of attention. Improvements in all phases of application are warmly welcomed by the user, and sampling of new products for testing proceeds at a lively pace.

Many companies have entered the field in recent years, and the existence of three sources for acrylic esters has served to stimulate activity among the specialty resin manufacturers. Borden's Polyco-monomer department is offering a series of acrylic copolymer emulsions for paint and paper. The Catalin Corp., long known as a producer of phenolics and other thermosets, has an extensive line of emulsions for the leather, textile, paint and adhesives market. Staley Chemical has recently combined forces with Union Bay State and has available products for paper and textiles. Polyvinyl Chemicals has concentrated its activity in the floor wax emulsion field. Reichhold Chemicals and Jersey State Chemical Co. are also manufacturing acrylic emulsions. In a number of cases, large users for a particular application are manufacturing the emulsions themselves. Rohm & Haas, the leader in the emulsion field, is also a manufacturer of a group of acrylic solution polymers. Catalin, a recent entry in this phase, also has developed an extensive line of thermoplastic and cross-linkable solution polymers.

With the field as active as this, it is expected that new resins and applications will be forthcoming at a rapid rate.

It was stated earlier that hundreds of acrylic monomers are available in experimental quantities. The search for new monomers still continues and from time to time a new one is added to the list. If a particular organic configuration appears to have interesting properties, many new compounds that are related to it are investigated. Acrylic monomers containing fluorine have lately undergone intensive investigation. It was found that elastomers containing fluorine had excellent high heat resistance. Under an Air Force contract the Minnesota Mining and Manufacturing Co. has investigated this possibility. Many patents have been issued that cover the work and some success has been attained using polymers derived from dihydroperfluorobutyl acrylate.

Acrolein and acrolein dimer and other intermediates based on acrylic aldehyde have been suggested for many uses in resins. Properties of its homopolymer and some copolymers have been investigated, and rubber-like polymers have been obtained by condensing acrolein with a haloprene. Large and small companies and university laboratories are investigating possible uses for many of the lesser-known monomers and their polymers. The field has intriguing possibilities for the research worker.

Graft polymerization is another wide-open field. Work to date has just scratched the surface and the first graft polymer products are just getting to the application testing phase. Some graft polymer work has been conducted with methyl methacrylate as part of the polymer, but much will be done in the near future to get more understanding of the possibilities of the process. A little-used type of catalyst has recently been revived as an interesting method of polymerization. The cyanoacrylate adhesive mentioned previously is a solventless anionic catalyzed polymer. Its unusual properties will certainly renew activity in this field.

When, in the past, conservative workers in the plastics field have been asked what the future will bring, their answer has frequently been a gross underestimation of actual events. Despite this, an honest statement of the future of acrylics would be: growth, not spectacular, but steady.

Appendix
SELECTED READING MATERIAL

The listings given here are far from all-inclusive, but will give the reader a comprehensive group of publications from which much information can be obtained on the various phases of the subject matter that has been covered.

Books: Coverage of the subject of acrylics in texts is rather sparse and no single treatise on the subject has been written.

"Vinyl and Related Polymers," Calvin E. Schildknecht, John Wiley & Sons, Inc., 1952. Chapters IV and V contain a great deal of general information on acrylics.

"Emulsion—Theory and Practice," Paul Becher, Reinhold Publishing Corp., 1957. This is not specifically directed to emulsion polymerization but chapters 2 and 6 discuss general theory that is of interest.

"Emulsion Polymerization," Bovey *et al.*, 1955, and "Copolymerization," Alfrey, Bohrer and Mark, 1952, published by Interscience Publishers. These two books deal with the theoretical aspects of their subjects in detail. Although they are of general interest, they are directed to the professional involved with this work.

"Monomeric Acrylic Esters," E. H. Riddle, Reinhold Publishing Corp., 1954. The properties of the acrylic monomers are covered in detail. Polymerization and copolymerization and control testing are discussed. An extensive bibliography makes this a valuable information source.

Journals: Among the many journals that carry articles on acrylics from time to time, a few are of more than passing interest:

Modern Plastics
Modern Plastics Encyclopedia (yearly)
Chemical and Engineering News
Industrial Finishing
Soap and Chemical Specialties
American Dyestuff Reporter
Chemical Processing

Many larger suppliers of monomers and polymers publish house organs on a regular basis, which frequently contain application information. Among these, mention should be made of the *Rohm & Haas Reporter,* and the *Acrylo-News* (American Cyanamid, Petrochemicals Department).

The basic information sources, of perhaps the greatest value in the applications field, are the "Industrial Arts Index" and "Chemical Abstracts." These comprehensive abstracts refer the user to the original article, patent or government publication. It is often well worth the effort to obtain the original article from the abstract.

Much statistical and experimental data are available from government publications. A listing of such publications and the publications themselves are available from the Superintendent of Documents, Washington, D.C.

Product Bulletins: The application chemist's primary source of information is the large variety of product bulletins issued by the suppliers of raw materials. These bulletins contain a wealth of data and information, ranging from theoretical considerations to basic application methods for a specific end use. Following is a list of some of these bulletins:

American Cyanamid Company
    The Reactions of Acrylonitrile With Halogens
    Chemistry of Acrylamide

Acrylonitrile, Polymers and Copolymers
Polyacrylamide
Creslan—Acrylic Fibers
Borden Chemical Company
Polyco—Acrylic Emulsion Polymers
Acrylic Ester and Acrylonitrile Rubber
Cadillac Plastics and Chemical Corp.
Cadco—Extruded Sheet
Carbide and Carbon Chemical Company
Acrolein
Acrylonitrile
Cast Optics Corporation
Evercleer—Cast Acrylics
Catalin Corporation of America
1100 Series—Acrylic Solution Polymers
1300 Series—Acrylic Emulsion Polymers
Chemstrand Corporation
Acrilan—Acrylic Fibers
Dow Chemical Company
Zerion 150—Molding Powder
Latex 2647—Acrylic Coatings
Tyril 767—Acrylonitrile Molding Compound
DuPont de Nemours & Company, Inc.
Lucite—Acrylic Resins
Orlon—Acrylic Fibers
Goodrich Chemical Company
Hycar—Acrylic Rubber
Goodyear Tire & Rubber Company
Chemigum Latex—Acrylonitrile Rubber
Heresite and Chemical Company
Herecrol—Acrylonitrile Rubber
Jersey State Chemical Company
Crilicron—Emulsion Polymers

Polyvinyl Chemicals, Inc.
  Neocryl—Acrylic Emulsions
Reichhold Chemicals, Inc.
  Synthemul—Acrylic Emulsions
Rohm & Haas Company
  Acryloid—Solution Polymers
  Rhoplex—Emulsion Polymers
  Acrysols—Water Soluble Polymers
  Plexiglas—Cast Sheet and Molding Compounds
  Implex—High-Impact Molding Compounds
Shell Chemical Corporation
  Acrolein
Staley Manufacturing Company
  Stacrylic—Emulsion Polymers
UBS Chemical Corporation
  Ubatol—Acrylic Emulsion Polymers
U.S. Rubber Corporation, Naugatuck Chemical Div.
  Kralastic—Acrylonitrile Rubber Molding Compounds
Wasco Company
  Acrylite—Decorative Cast Sheet

INDEX

Acrolein
  formula, 16
  synthesis, 22
Acrylamide
  formula, 16
  synthesis, 22
Acrylic acid
  formula, 2, 16
  physical properties, 17
  synthesis, 21
"Acryloid," 15
Acrylonitrile
  formula, 16
  in ester synthesis, 20
  physical properties, 21
  synthesis, 21
Acrylonitrile-butadiene rubber,
    153, 154-155
Adhesives
  acrylic, 146-148
  pressure sensitive, 7
Aircraft products, 78
Annealing
  cast products, 78
  cast sheet, 41
Architectural products, 78
Azo-type catalysts, 26

Back coating of pile fabrics, 136
Benzoin, polymerization catalyst,
    26

Benzoyl peroxide, polymerization
    catalyst, 26, 27
Block polymers, 32
Bulk casting, procedure, 40-41, 43
Bulk polymerization, 26-27
  factors, 33-36
  in water bath, 40
  raw materials, 35

Cast products, 78-83
  annealing, 78
  machining, 58-60
  manufacturers of, 11-12
  new developments, 166-167
Cast rods, 44
Cast rods and tubes, sizes, 48
Cast sheet
  annealing, 41
  cementing, 71-72
  coefficient of expansion, 58
  cutting, 55-57
    by band saw, 56
    by circular saw, 55
  die cutting, 57
  finishing, 75-77
    ashing, 77
  forming
    air pressure differential, 69
    blow back, 67
    deep drawing, 66
    drape, 67

Cast sheet—(*Cont.*)
    factors, 60-67
    heating cycles, 61
    heating methods, 62
    methods, 67-71
    molds, 67
    preheated molds, 63
    shrinkage, 66
    temperatures, 64
  machining with shaper and router, 59
  masking, 42, 53
  parts assembly, 71-75
  rod and tube
    distributors, 53
    manufacturers, 52
    properties, 47
  sanding, buffing and polishing, 75
  sizes and tolerances, 48
  spray masking, 54
  storage and handling, 53-54
  tapping and threading, 60
  types and sources, 51-53
Casting
  specialty sheet, rods and tubes, 45-46
  with monomer-polymer slurry, 46
Casting cell, in bulk polymerization, 36-38
Castings, improvement by crosslinking, 49
Cast tubes, 43
Catalysts, 26, 27
  azo-type, 26
  free radical type, 26
  polymerization, 26, 34, 105
Cementing, cast sheet, 71-72
Chain transfer agents, 24
Copolymerization, methods, 31

Copolymers
  crosslinking with, 10
  general, 9-10
  with other than acrylics, 31
Cost factors, monomers, 9, 162
Crosslinking, to improve castings, 49
Crosslinking agents, 24
Cutting, cast sheet, 55-57

Decorating, moldings and extrusions, 99-100
Dental restorations, 47
Depolymerization, 46
Display items, from bulk castings, 80

Elastomers
  acrylic based, 152-156
  from acrylonitrile, 5
  manufacturers, 13
Embedments, in castings, 156-157
Emulsifiers, in polymerization, 28
Emulsion paints, 139-143
  formulation, 142
Emulsion polymerization, 28, 102-105
  agitation, 111
  catalysts, 105
  laboratory apparatus, 110
  laboratory example, 112
  mechanism, 102
  monomers, 104
  pH control, 108
  surfactants, 105-108
  under redox, 108
  under reflux, 108
Emulsion polymers
  compared to solution, 100
  in textile treatment, 5
  manufacturers, 13

Emulsions
  chemical stability, 128
  evaluation, 123-128
  for paper coating, 6, 137-139
  freeze-thaw resistance, 127
  future trends, 173-174
  mechanical stability, 126
  particle size, 125
  viscosity, 124
Ethyl acrylate
  in transesterification, 18
  physical constants, 20
Ethylene, use in monomer synthesis, 21
Evaluation
  of emulsions, 123-128
  polymer films, 128-133
Exotherm, in bulk polymerization, 34
Exothermic heat, in polymerization, 26
Extruded products, producers, 99
Extrusion, sheets and forms, 97-99

Fibers, 158-162
  "Acrilan," 160
  "Dynel," 162
  flow sheet, 161
  "Orlon," 162
  properties, 160
Films of polymers
  abrasion resistance, 131
  blocking, 131
  evaluation, 128-133
  gloss, 130
  graininess, 130
  solvent resistance, 132
  surface hardness, 130
  water resistance, 132
Finishing, cast sheet, 75-77

Floor waxes, from synthetic polymers, 143
Forming, cast sheet, 60-71
Formulas
  methacrylic acid, 2, 16
  methyl acrylate, 16
  methyl methacrylate, 16
  structural, monomers, 16
Formulation
  emulsion paint, 142
  paper coating, 138

"Gafite" cast sheet, 49
Gasket, in casting cell, 37
Graft polymerization, 175
Graft polymers, 32
Granulation polymerization, 29, 87

Hill, Dr. Rowland, 15
History of polymers, 10-11
Homopolymers, 30
Hydroquinine, monomer inhibitor, 25

Imperial Chemical Industries, 15
"Implex," modified molding compound, 168
  properties chart, 169
Inhibiting of monomers, 25
Inhibitors, removal, 25, 35
Injection molding, 91-96
Injection molds, design, 93

Lacquers, from solution polymers, 143
Laminating syrup, 170
Leather base coatings, from emulsions, 7, 144-146
"Lucite," molding powder, 90

Machining, cast products, 58-60
Mercaptans, as chain transfer agents, 25
Methacrylic acid
  formula, 2, 16
  synthesis, 21
Methyl acrylate
  formula, 16
  physical constants, 20
  synthesis, 18
Methyl ether of hydroquinine, as monomer inhibitor, 25
Methyl methacrylate
  curing curve, 39
  formula, 16
  physical constants, 20
  synthesis, 17-18
Molding compound, modified "Implex," 168
Molding powder
  drying, 91
  early products, 84
  "Lucite," 90
  "Plexiglas," 90
  properties, 90
  property chart, 88
Molecular weight
  effect on polymer, 24
  measurement, 125
Monomer-polymer slurry, in casting, 46
Monomers
  acrylic, general, 1
  as chemical intermediates, 2, 23
  commercial sources, 11
  cost factors, 9, 162
  higher homologs, 17
  in emulsion polymerization, 104
  in solution polymerization, 114

new plants, 164-165
structural formulas, 16
substituted, 2, 17
synthesis by transesterification, 18
Monomers and polymers, historical, 14-15

Non-woven fabrics, bonding, 136

Oil additives, 157-158
Oxygen, inhibiting effect, 25

Paint, emulsion based, 6, 139-143
Paper coating
  formulation, 138
  with emulsions, 6, 137-139
"Perspex," 15
Physical constants
  ethyl acrylate, 20
  methyl acrylate, 20
  methyl methacrylate, 20
Physical properties, acrylic acid, 17
Plasticization, internal, 8
"Plexiglas"
  cast sheet, 51
  molding powder, 90
Polyacrylamide, 150
Polyacrylic acid, 149
Polymer chains, types, 30-32
Polymerization
  catalysts, 26, 34
  chemistry of, 23-26
  granular, 29
  in bulk, 26-27
    under pressure, 27, 43
  in emulsion, 28, 102-105
  in solution, 27
  in suspension, 29, 85-90
  types, 2, 26-29

Polymers
  acrylic, general properties and products, 3-7
  block, 32
  history, 10-11
  physical property range, 24
  production figures, 165-166
  solution, 6
  water soluble, 6, 149-152
Prepolymer syrup, 36
Production, of polymers, 165-166
Products from bulk castings, 78-83
  aircraft, 78
  architectural, 78
  displays, 80
  signs, 80
Properties
  acrylonitrile, 21
  acrylonitrile-butadiene rubber, 153
  cast sheet rod and tube, 47
  of fibers, 160
Properties chart, "Implex," 169
Property charts, cast and molded acrylics, 94-96

Redox, in polymerization, 108
Rohm, Dr. Otto, 15
Rohm & Haas, A. G., 15
Rubber, based on acrylic esters, 156

Sales, total 1957, 9
Shrinkage, during polymerization, 35
Signs, from cast products, 80
Sodium polyacrylate, 151
Solution polymerization, 27, 117-121
  catalysts, 118

effect of temperature, 117
  example, 120-121
  experimental reactor, 119
  monomers, 114
  solvents, 115-116
Solution polymers
  as lacquer coatings, 143
  manufacturers, 12
Solvents, in solution polymerization, 115-116
Surfactants, in emulsion polymerization, 105-108
Suspension polymerization, 29, 85-90
  factors in, 85
Synthesis
  acrylamide, 22
  acrylic acid, 21
  acrylonitrile, 21
  acrolein, 22
  catalytic, of lower esters, 21
  methacrylic acid, 21
  methyl acrylate, 18
  methyl methacrylate, 17-18
Synthetic fibers, from acrylonitrile, 5

Tempered glass, in casting cell, 37
Textile applications, 133
  back-coating of pile fabrics, 136
  bonding of non-woven fabrics, 136
  hand modifiers, 135
  permanent starch, 134
  with solution polymers, 137
Time-temperature, in bulk casting, 38-40
Toxicity of monomers, in manufacture, 22

Vinyl monomers, family of, 1-2